CW00595198

Introduction

There was a time when my fishing thoughts and plans were centred upon the River Wensum and the estate lakes and gravel pits of the beautiful valley between Norwich and Fakenham where I am fortunate to live. During this past year however it has only been possible for me to enjoy fishing close to home on quite rare occasions.

When I was looking back over this diary it seemed as though I had spent fewer days fishing than in previous years. Indeed, as much of my fishing is now geared either to researching or filming programmes for Anglia Television, I suggest (tongue firmly in cheek), that a proportion of this book might even be deemed work and therefore should not strictly come under the heading of fishing. Out of curiosity I decided to count up the number of days I actually fished during 1990 and look back into a diary book called *A Specimen Fishing Year* which I wrote in 1976. In that sweltering year I fished on no fewer than 103 days, compared to 79 in 1990. I may not fish quite so often these days but when I do I often travel half-way round the world for my sport. This year has seen me taking barracuda in the mangrove swamps of the Gambia River, fishing in a blizzard in Ireland, battling with the mighty mahseer in India, finding carp in unusual places in Spain, tracking down tuna off Maderia, pulling monster bags from the rivers of Denmark and then back in the Gambia grappling with huge sharks. In between I have revisited many of my favourite haunts in England, met up with some old friends and encouraged some new ones to take part in the sport which has given me so much. All in all I consider myself to be very fortunate.

The reader may wonder whether those blank days, common to every fisherman, were all included in this account. Let me assure him that every single day's fishing that I have had in 1990 has been faithfully logged; triumphs and disasters alike. I have had great pleasure in recording my experiences to share them in the pages of this book; I sincerely hope that the reader enjoys my year as much as I did.

John Wilson
Great Witchingham, 1991

Monday 1

*Heavily overcast and chilly
with a hint of rain.*

For the trotting enthusiast there is no finer way of brushing away the cobwebs and breaking in the New Year than travelling south to the clear blue chalkstreams of Hampshire and Berkshire in search of grayling. Unfortunately, brother Dave and I had over indulged the night before and could certainly have done without a raucous alarm call at 6 am when the party had only ended an hour earlier. Talk about feeling fragile.

In fact it was lucky we had decided not to see the old year out back in Norfolk, or a further two hours would have been added to the hour and a quarter drive from Dave's home in Hertfordshire down to Hampshire. At least the drive proved pleasant; never before have I seen the M25 so empty. Soon we were purring along the M3 and after a quick stop for coffee and a fry up we took the Andover road heading for a particularly pretty and secluded stretch of the upper Test. I have not visited this lovely river for several years and had even forgotten the final twisting route through tiny roads flanked on both sides by enticing carriers and water meadows. A quick call from a phone box to Terry the river keeper put us straight, and minutes later we were there, in a piece of England so peaceful and unspoilt, Dave found it difficult to take it all in. Terry climbed into the back of the car and directed us through muddy fields towards the bottom half of his four and a half mile beat, a fishery of which he is justly proud, with well-kept banks and a superb head of brown trout and large grayling. This ranks amongst the finest chalkstream fishing in the world and the syndicate members pay heavily for the privilege.

With fumbling fingers we made ready 13 foot trotting rods coupled to centrepins holding 2 lb test and chunky two swan shot loafer floats; a pouch full of maggots and brandlings belted around the waist completed the simplest of outfits. Ours was to be a wandering day; no stools or keepnets, holdalls or rod rests. Save for a hip flask apiece, only a few spare hooks, shots and floats lined our waistcoat pockets, leaving us free to roam up or down with the flow, as the mood took us. Terry unlocked the old thatched fishing lodge and bade us farewell until the afternoon. The walls of the lodge were lined with tracings on thin, varnished plywood of giant salmon taken from the river's lower beats many years ago; it

John Wilson's
GO FISHING
Year

As the presenter of GO FISHING and a prolific
angling writer, John Wilson has become
known to millions. He was born in Enfield, North
London in 1943. After a spell as a ladies'
hairdresser and merchant seaman he lived in the
West Indies for three years, then settled in
Norfolk where he has run a tackle shop in
Norwich for the last twenty years.
His books for Boxtree include the best-selling
Go Fishing, Wilson's Angle and the new coarse
fishing series for the Angling Times Library:
*Catch Carp, Catch Pike, Catch Chub, Catch Tench,
Catch Bream, Catch Barbel* and *Catch Roach, Rudd & Dace
with John Wilson.* He is also a regular contributor to
many angling magazines.
In his spare time John Wilson pursues his
interests in conservation, fisheries management
and photography.

ANGLIA
Television Limited

B⊞XTREE

A CHANNEL
FOUR BOOK

For Tania

A new year and a new beginning.

First published in the UK 1991 by

BOXTREE LIMITED
36 Tavistock Street
London WC2E 7PB

First paperback edition published in 1992

10 9 8 7 6 5 4 3 2 1

© (text and photographs) John Wilson 1991
© (illustrations) Boxtree Limited 1991

Illustrations by Dave Batten
Design by Dave Goodman/Millions Design

Set in 12/13pt Linotron Baskerville
Typeset by Cambrian Typesetters, Frimley, Surrey
Colour origination by Fotographics, Hong Kong
Printed and bound in Italy by Amadeus, Rome

Except in the United States of America,
this book is sold subject to the condition
that it shall not by way of trade or
otherwise, be lent, resold, hired out or
otherwise circulated without the publisher's
prior consent in any form of binding or
cover other than that in which it is
published and without a similar condition
including this condition being imposed on a
subsequent purchaser.

A catalogue record for this book is available from the
British Library

ISBN 1 85283 182 0

All rights reserved

Contents

was like being in a time machine, and Dave's face was an absolute picture. 'I've never seen anything like this before', he muttered. This was of course perfectly true; such privileges are increasingly rare.

We started our fishing at the junction pool where a deep carrier joins the main stream, taking a dozen or so nice grayling to around the pound on long trotted maggot and

Easing it gingerly upstream against a strong flow, brother David's first fish of 1990 is a superb grayling from Hampshire's enchanting River Test.

In the subtle hues of silver and violet enamel with their flecked, sail-like dorsal fins tipped in crimson, our grayling ranged from a few ounces to beauties topping 1½ lb. Coming regularly to maggots or brandlings long-trotted through fast water depressions, there was not a species nor a part of England we could have enjoyed more than this lady of the stream and the watercress meadows of Hampshire.

worm cocktails offered on a size 12 hook. For comparatively unfished grayling such as these, there was little point in decreasing the hook size. I had to remind Dave that this was a roaming day, and drag him away from that first swim, such was his fascination and excitement. We then started a slow meander towards the top of the fishery, trying every little nook and cranny en route. Narrow runs along the near bank between beds of weed still unbelievably green; deep holes on the bends where quite suddenly, depth increases from one to over three feet; clear runs beneath overhanging alders and willows; runs beneath foot bridges; scoured-out junctions where drainage dykes and mini carriers enter the river. Our floats eagerly explored them all, and we soon lost count. Interspersed with the occasional out-of-season brownie, quickly unhooked in the water, grayling of all sizes came our way from just a few ounces to deep-bodied beauties of 1½ lb. Their sail-like dorsal fins marked in peacock blue with an edge of crimson, as only chalkstream grayling are.

Next only to trotting my beloved River Wensum for roach, I love wandering for grayling perhaps more than any other technique. It is a method of which one never tires, because around every corner is a new swim, a new challenge, a different approach, an unknown shoal.

At around 3 pm the drizzle that had been threatening all day started up and slowly dampened our enthusiasm, so we trudged back to the car, weary but happy. Of the 80–90 grayling taken, at least 30 would have easily topped the pound. Once again the tiny River Test had treated its visitors like lords.

After thanking Terry for his generosity, we set off in the direction of Newbury with the rain lashing down outside. Making the journey in good time we found a guest house on the ring road and after a hot shower, popped into town to end the day with an Indian meal. By 8 pm we were back at the digs and fast asleep.

This morning we breakfasted at 7 am on sausage, tomatoes, eggs and toast, before loading the car up and following the course of the Kennet upstream along the old A4 road, to where a good friend keeps a wonderful trout fishery. David Culley and I really do enjoy each other's fishing. He pops up to Norfolk periodically to fish my carp lakes, whilst I love nothing better than roaming his five miles of the Kennet armed with trotting tackle during the winter months. It is a truly superb stretch, split into several interesting little sections. There are narrow carriers and small pools as well as three deep weir pools on the main river itself; there is even a length of an old canal.

It is the kind of fishery where you never know what's going to grab hold next. Although it is primarily a well-kept syndicate fishery stocked with equal numbers of brown and rainbow trout, this part of the Kennet does breed an exceptionally fine head of coarse fish: roach, perch, huge dace, chub, pike and even the odd carp which migrates in from the adjacent canal, not to mention a strong head of quality grayling.

2 Tuesday

Chilly, sky clear at times after sharp overnight frost. Windy.

Watched by brother David and river keeper David Culley, Bruce Vaughan prepares the net in readiness for a big roach, but yet another out-of-season spotty thrashes the surface.

Fortified by the customary tipple, the Wilson brothers plan their morning's ramble along the River Kennet.

As arranged, we arrived promptly on David's doorstep at 8 am to be given a warm hug by his mum Madge, who soon had the tea on while we nattered about conditions and prospects for the day. My old mate Bruce Vaughan of Wychwood Tackle arrived from Oxford shortly after us, and soon we were all following the river's course down from the house along the very stretch where only a year earlier I had made one of the programmes in series four of *Go Fishing*. Conditions appeared quite similar to that day, though a chilly wind ruffled the surface of the main river. In retrospect, sport would have been more consistent had we concentrated on dace and grayling in the shallow, narrow carriers and smaller pools. But our thoughts were with the large roach inhabiting the deeps at the end of the fishery in the wide water immediately above the end weir; a section varying in depth between six and ten feet.

Bruce and I had caught roach to over 2 lb here during the previous winter, but never really felt that we had come to grips with the river. This is obviously the case when you put in just a single day's fishing out of the blue. The challenge is to make the most of things and brother Dave did just this, hooking and subsequently beating on 2 lb test, a superbly conditioned out-of-season brown trout of over 6 lb. This fish came on brandlings trotted around the swirling waters of the pool itself which Dave continued to flog all morning while Bruce and I weighed up the roaching prospects, sadly to no avail. By lunchtime when we all trudged back to the house for a superb pheasant roast, we had accounted for numbers of grayling to the pound, plus a few nuisance trout, to long-trotted maggots on size 16 hooks. The big roach and even the dace, which are usually very active, were conspicuous by their absence. The grayling were shy too, giving nothing like their characteristic bold bites; they wanted the bait twitched by holding the float back sharply for a second or two, before showing any interest at all. Very few bites materialised from allowing the chunky loafer floats to trot through steadily. As an insurance policy I had baited the deepest run on a bend immediately below an overhanging alder just before we went in for lunch with half a loaf of mashed bread, and it was into this swim, bellies now full of pheasant, that Dave and I settled for the last hour before darkness filled the valley. This proved to have been a wise move, as small baits on small hooks to fine lines proved ineffective. Bruce and keeper David concentrated their efforts in a similar swim upstream on the opposite bank, where they took several nice dace to around the 12 oz mark plus one small chub, all on quiver tipped maggots as the light faded. The roach however were not having any.

Had our one and only loaf been fresh, the quiver tipped flake might have stayed on the hook longer (yes, it's a poor excuse) and I rather suspect the odd nice roach might have come our way. As it was, bites were mere single 'rustles' on the tip, even after fishing a good hour into darkness; proving that the fish were indeed present in the swim but not really switched on aggressively. Eventually, in frustration, I changed over to a cube of breadcrust which held on better, and quickly took a chub of exactly 4 lb. For the following hour gentle bites continued from what I suspected were quality roach, but all proved unhittable, so at 6.30 pm with the temperature dropping fast we trudged wearily back to the house for a warm up. This was one of those exasperating sessions where you find yourself questioning your tactics for days afterwards. Eventually you come to terms with the fact that a pig's ear was made of the situation.

Highlight of the day for us all, though a regular pleasure for keeper David, was the sight of the honey-coloured short eared owl quartering the lonely marshlands full of tussock sedge and soft rush an hour before dusk.

SALT WATER TROPICS

5-12

Sunny most days all day with temperatures in the high 80°s. Gentle breeze at times. Gusty off shore.

Cramming one whole week of exploratory, tropical sea fishing into a single entry is not easy. But as I must start somewhere, let's take the run up prior to our 767 leaving Gatwick Airport. Martin Founds and I travelled down the evening before to stay in a nearby hotel in order to meet a 5 am check-in – we were taking no chances with this flight; our Gambia expedition had been planned and eagerly anticipated over a long period of time.

Martin had in fact suggested we team up several years ago in order to expand his *Anglers World Holidays* business. As a

tour operator, he arranges all the flights and hotels and liaises with the various tourist and government bodies, while my job is to concentrate on the photography and writing, not to mention the fishing research. This provides the words and pictures for his brochure and also builds up my own portfolio of photographs for possible use in future articles and books. It is a partnership which has evolved into a strong friendship and it works very well indeed. Besides, it gets me away from the tackle shop every now and then.

The Gambia is wedge-shaped and relatively small as African countries go, bordered on both its north and south by Senegal. I had in fact fished several times at Dakar, which is due north of the Gambia in French-speaking Senegal, over 20 years ago when I was in the Merchant Navy. The fishing then was both varied and exciting to a young Londoner, with everything on offer from sharks to the tiniest, most colourful of coral reef fishes. The situation is not dissimilar where the

Against a background of oyster-encrusted mangrove roots, a heron wades in the mud at low tide, searching for the rich pickings provided by the Gambia River.

The wide mangrove-lined tidal channels fed by the mighty Gambia River contain a galaxy of exotic, beautifully coloured tropical sea fishes. Martin Founds accounted for this powerful red snapper using cut fish bait ledgered on freshwater tackle.

Gambia River enters the sea by the capital Banjul. The main difference is that the Gambia River, being several hundred miles long and freshwater in its upper reaches, continually brings down an enormous amount of sediment. Thus for up to 40 miles off-shore from the mouth, which is some ten miles wide at Banjul, one encounters huge areas of shallow sand banks, right up until the steep drop into deep blue water. By contrast, in Dakar blue water and the associated pelagic bill fishes such as marlin and sailfish are easily and quickly reached.

Nevertheless the Gambia river and its coastline has a wealth of fishing to offer, not to mention the mysterious, endless maze of mangrove-fringed creeks and channels where the coloured water varies between six and twenty feet deep. The potential of areas such as these cries out to trolling enthusiasts, to those who love to fish cut bait or whole fish at anchor, and even those wishing to spin from the shore. Such is the variety within the complex of creeks alone, that a man could spend his entire life striving to come to grips with it. Martin and I had but six days to sample a little of everything.

Needless to say continuous and lively sport with an endless supply of weird and wonderful species kept us more than fascinated. Beneath a blazing sun in an average midday temperature of 90° (raw blisters along my neck still hurt as I write one week later) we sampled trolling for barracuda in the narrow, winding mangrove creeks using large diving rapalas. We hired a local wooden boat to anchor at the creek junctions where depth increases, and fished cut bait for the delicious and beautifully coloured red snappers. An off-shore boat was chartered to fish with big baits at anchor in the deep channel of the river mouth for shark, catfish and rays. We soon struck a wonderful rapport with the two northerners Mark and Graham who operate on charter *White Warrior*, a 32 foot sports fishing boat complete with navigational equipment and fighting chairs. In poor fishing conditions (even the local fishermen said things were bad), they really worked hard to put us onto something big by trying several anchorages out in the mouth of the river where depth varied between 40 and 60 feet over smooth and rough ground.

All week long a school of over 100 friendly porpoises ploughed up and down the river entrance, providing us with some wonderful sights of acrobatic agility as they cavorted between the local fishing boats also at anchor fishing cut bait for a living. Mark and Graham attributed the poor fishing to the presence of these amiable creatures, and I was inclined to agree. Even with a huge batch of rubby dubby made from hundreds of cut fish, oil, blood and guts, we failed to attract more than the passing complement of reef fishes, snappers and catfish. I did part company on a heavy outfit with something ripping line off healthily, but the line fractured against the coral. Nevertheless we experienced enough action

Enjoying the mystery of 'bran tub' fishing at its very best, John grips the side of the dinghy for support whilst bending his carp rod heavily into an unseen inhabitant of the mangroves. Anything from stingrays to snappers and even small barracuda are on offer when presenting small, whole fish dead baits on the bottom.

with a variety of great battlers. I particularly liked the casarva, a zander-like fish sporting two dorsal fins and a shimmering silver livery, which is said to reach 40 lb. On a medium spinning rod coupled to 15 lb test, I found casarva to around 12 lb quite enough to handle. This of course is the recipe for true salt water enjoyment, using tackle which allows what you catch to show its mettle, instead of using a meat stick outfit just in case a whopper turns up. You are then not so bothered if a big sleeping outfit remains inactive. A big stingray which can average over 100 lb just offshore, or one of the lemon sharks which top 300 lb would have been a

Graham, John and Mark Longster (skipper of White Warrior), *display the fruits of just an hour's trolling with deep diving rapalas through the mangrove creeks between Denton Bridge and the Gambia River mouth at Banjul Harbour.*

Coloured in metallic shades of silver and pewter and not unlike the European zander – even down to the twin dorsal fins – this pair of casarva fell to fish fillet presented off-shore in the mouth of the Gambia River.

welcome addition, but both will have to wait for our next visit. As it was, I think that what I enjoyed most was the challenge of presenting static dead baits at anchor in the creeks for barracuda, of which there are three separate species. The 700 would squeal like crazy on the ratchet in free spool as a 'cuda shot off with a small whole mullet mounted on a wire trace, size 6/0 hook and just a 2 ounce bomb – almost pike fishing! But these seemingly unmissable runs were missed time and time again on the large single. Next time I'll try a brace or three trebles in the mullet; although this may well deter a ray or big snapper from picking it up, it will certainly account for a higher percentage of barracuda landed to those hooked. Anyone owning a pike outfit can easily enjoy this creek sport because a local boat is so cheap to rent. As most of the species come armed with wicked teeth, a wire trace is imperative, but line strength should be no more than 12–15 lb test, with size 2–2/0 hooks for cut bait. The best barracuda from the mangrove channels, where fiddler crabs peek from holes in the mud at low tide and oysters festoon the vertical roots, was taken by Martin on a trolled rapala. It looked so much larger than 14 lb when compared to a pike of the same weight, almost twice as long in fact, and fought incredibly hard. Its teeth are pretty frightening and you never mess about trying to extract the hooks until the fish is safely dispatched. Cleaned, skinned and cut into two inch steaks, barracuda is improved if marinated in fresh lime juice for two hours before cooking. This tenderises and completely changes the texture of the meat. The steaks should then be dried on kitchen paper and deep incisions made, into which finely chopped onion is pressed. Finally they are heavily seasoned in black pepper, rolled in cornflour and slowly pan-fried till golden brown. Talk about delicious – I feel hungry simply writing about this old West Indian recipe, which is suitable for cooking any fish from which steaks can be cut.

We found that hotels in the Gambia are of an exceptionally high standard. All offer a full entertainments programme throughout the week, though all we had time to enjoy, having fished all day, was the dinner dancing and late-night discos. The best beach fishing was immediately outside the Sunwing Hotel, between some long rocky outcrops, where species from catfish to rays come close in shore during the cover of

darkness. There is also a good chance of taking big fish at night from Denton Road Bridge which spans one of the creeks just south of Banjul. During the rainy season from June through to August even tarpon can be hooked from the bridge along with barracuda, rays, snappers, small sharks, ladyfish and a whole host of other toothy species. Locals use heavy handlines from the bridge, but most whoppers find sanctuary around the barnacle-covered supports; Martin and I spent a few hours rowing around the supports beneath the bridge using a Humminbird fish finder and located some good sized shoals. I suspect that anyone drifting a big bait well out and away from the bridge on the ebbing tide could hook and probably land something of large proportions.

Along with the fishing, the bird life on the Gambia River is also quite stunning – the very first bird I saw fly over the boat on our trip was an osprey and the second was a pelican. Vultures roam the thermals high overhead all day long, and around the mangroves herons and other wading birds abound in all sorts of shapes, colours and sizes. We saw pied kingfishers and oyster catchers and one evening laid eyes upon an old green-back turtle, lifting its head slowly every so often as it leisurely drifted into the creek on top of the making tide. We took time off one morning to visit the Abuko Wildlife Park which includes an incredible collection of exotic jungle trees, palms and climbers plus wild flowers of every colour imaginable. In the middle of the reserve there is a small zoo; ironically we discovered that its four lions were in fact donated from Longleat! Monkeys honk and squabble in the high treetops as you walk through the pleasantly cool and dark jungle paths, while down on the floor a thousand rustles through dry leaves signify the presence of lizards, snakes and rodents. Exquisite butterflies flit to and fro, while the tiniest of brightly coloured nectar-sipping birds hover against flowers. We also made an interesting short stop at the crocodile pond, a popular attraction on the outskirts of Banjul, where tourists are invited to stroke and play with a large tame croc. It looked decidedly stuffed, but as I wasn't entirely sure, Martin gingerly stroked its tail while I clicked away on the end of the zoom lens. Slowly one eye opened and

Charlie, the tame 'croc', lives in a lily-filled pool on the outskirts of Banjul, capital of The Gambia, where visitors are encouraged to stroke and even feed him fish scraps by hand.

closed, to prove that respect was necessary even for such an obviously well-fed predator.

I could have sat out at sea in deep water just shark fishing all week, or spent the entire stay exploring the mangroves further inland, perhaps even following the Gambia River into its freshwater reaches in search of a whole new galaxy of species. There is certainly more than enough exciting material to feature the Gambia in a TV fishing programme – the problem would be deciding what to leave out! We were told that October and early November during the flat water period following the rainy season is best for all-round sport, so perhaps Martin and I will return for further research in this fascinating country later in the year.

After going barefoot all week wearing nothing more than shorts, enjoying the freedom this affords the human mind, I really did not fancy boarding the plane back to Gatwick and a British downpour. I left thinking that maybe in a few years I will return to the tropics to live permanently.

Sunday 21

Mild and cloudy with occasional sunny periods. Stiff westerly breeze.

It took a nostalgic journey back through several years of fishing diaries to recall when I last took my 19-year-old son, Lee, pike fishing. In fact it was six years ago and by coincidence we had fished the same deep lake near Norwich that was our destination today.

In Norfolk we are blessed with a variety of excellent pike fishing sites, not only throughout the tidal river and broadland system, but also in the numerous pits, estate lakes and meres which drain into many of the small upper rivers. It was at the mysterious 'Conifers' Lake, so named due to the tall evergreens, cedars and pine, which dwarf the oaks along its northern bank, that Lee and I set our sights for a big pike, anchoring the boat bows into the stiff westerly some 60 yards from the reedy eastern shoreline. The shallow margins of the lake are heavily overgrown with tall reeds or a mixture of alders and willow, the depth then plunges quickly away down to between 12 and 15 feet, remaining fairly constant across the entire lake from bank to bank.

Around 15 acres of superb pike fishing are created and sustained by an enormous concentration of fodder fish in roach, rudd, perch and skimmer bream of all age groups. Even the dozen or so cormorants that have overwintered on the lake during the past two years, seem to have had little effect on the balance. As yet! When the water goes clear after continual sharp frosts, deep diving plugs and spinner baits can really produce the goods. But whenever wind churns up the sediment reducing visibility to a mere foot or so, deadbaits presented either wobbled, or better still fished perfectly static on the bottom, reign supreme for the larger pike. Due to the gusty breeze we decided to dispense with floats altogether, opting for simple freelined tactics with three swan shot added to the trace holding a brace of size 8 semi-barbless trebles. These shots help keep the bait truly static, and give the pike a little something to pull against. Runs therefore are nearly always positive 'away from the boat' pulls. It is lovely to watch the loop of line, held in an elastic band above the reel, suddenly and audibly pull out, and line evaporate from the open spool. This is what winter deadbaiting is all about, and the first text book run came around 10 am, within minutes of the sun peeking through heavy cloud cover. On this deep, coloured lake pike are often spurred into foraging by sudden

increases in light values; down there in the murky depths it must be like someone switching on the electric light in a darkened room, when strong sunlight replaces grey skies. Lee allowed the pike a few yards, then wound down and banged it as hard as the 11 lb test would permit, while Dad cleared the other rods ready for action. I need not have bothered, this particular pike – a plump female of around 12 lb – must have been on the booze the night before because it allowed Lee to crank it almost straight to the surface. Only then did it thrash and try a couple of dives beneath the boat. This was a good start and Lee's face produced an ear-to-ear grin as we settled down to the waiting game again. Two rods were positioned fishing whole smelt up into the wind, with mackerel tails on

The first time I saw the monstrous proportions of Lee's pike, wallowing on the surface close to the boat, was through the camera lens.

23

On a bitterly cold and windy day happiness is obviously pike-shaped for Lee Wilson. This beautifully marked specimen took the dial scales round to 23 lb 12 oz. Dad bagged a six pounder at the end of the day.

the two downwind rods. It wasn't a case of Lee's rods and my rods, because on our last visit six years back, when the pike were really going potty, I hit a run on Lee's second rod while he was messing with a tangle and small fish on the other, and promptly boated a 21 pounder, a fish I dearly would have loved Lee to catch. So today, I suggested he hit all the runs while I stayed on the camera, in the hope a biggy might show. This is exactly what happened – how I wish such events would materialise so conveniently during the filming of a TV programme!

One of the downwind mackerel tails was taken and by the look of the curve on Lee's 12 foot 2 lb test carbon, which stayed alarmingly bent after putting the hooks home, this was no low double. Slowly line was taken against the fairly tight clutch, creating that lovely wind whine. For an occasional angler, I must give Lee his due, because he played that fish sensibly and without haste, allowing it to run wherever it wished under full, steady pressure. The first time I actually saw its size was through the camera lens while filming a sequence of the pike wallowing on the surface close to the boat. I instantly blurted out 'that's a bloody great 20 pounder Lee'. This unfortunately put the pressure on, and he had a real job bundling it into the landing net against the gusting wind, but in it went just the same. More action shots on the Bronica of heaving the fish over the gunnel followed and by its sheer physical size as it lay in the bottom of the small dinghy, I instantly put its weight at over 25 lb; however the scales said 23 lb 12 oz. The pleasure and firmness of Lee's handshake could only have been so well understood and enjoyed by his now totally ecstatic father.

Later on, just before we pulled the mudweights up at 3 pm, I had a bang on a wobbled smelt from a jack of about 6 lb, and apart from two dropped runs following the capture of Lee's monster, that was it. By Conifers standards this was a fairly slow day in numbers of fish, but for Lee a most memorable occasion indeed.

I very much enjoyed this rare trip out together, because as he gets older Lee seems less interested in fishing. Perhaps I rammed it down his throat too much during childhood, always taking him to where I was catching big fish at the time, so he caught them too, instead of taking time out for netting tiddlers. Before the age of seven, Lee had caught perch over 2 lb and tench of 6 lb plus. Sadly none of us can go back, though there are occasions when as a father I would dearly love to. What a wonderful day.

Tuesday 23

Sunny all day. Strong to gale force westerly wind.

While we were in the Gambia, Martin Founds asked whether I fancied a two day trip over to Northern Ireland later on in the month to sample the fabulous sport with big roach and hybrids, which migrate into the River Bann at Toome Bridge at this time of the year. It was an invitation I could not resist now that I had taken on my friend Andy Jubb as full time manager of the tackle shop. Particularly since the party included some old mates from up north – ex-world champion Kevin Ashurst, eccentric tackle dealer John Roberts from Lancashire and Terry Smith and Ray Bows from Sheffield. We have teamed up regularly in recent years with Martin on research trips to many parts of Ireland and to Sweden, and had such a ball especially when out on the town in the evenings that the fishing has at times seemed almost secondary. If it achieves nothing else, fishing brings people together from different walks of life and forges lasting friendships. Living close to the ferry ports all the lads went overnight by sea and then picked me up from Belfast

Airport, from which our accommodation, the O'Neill Arms Hotel at Toome Bridge, was only a 20 minute drive away.

It is strange that most of the anglers visiting Ireland go straight to the south, because there is a wealth of really excellent potential in the north, particularly on the river Blackwater and the mighty Bann. Both flow into the southern end of Lough Neagh, which at 154 square miles is the largest sheet of freshwater in the British Isles. The Bann then exits from Neagh following a northerly course and flows beneath Toome Bridge where a complicated system of lock gates and traps built across the entire width of the river create an enormous salmon and eel fishing industry. So large is the annual tonnage of adult eels trapped here (most are smoked and sold in Europe) that Father Kennedy who runs the eel fishery, actually imports millions of young elvers from the River Severn each year for stocking into Loch Neagh.

Our main interest on this trip was the migration of quality roach and enormous roach/bream hybrids, plus the occasional large bream, which exist in the Bann anywhere from Toome Bridge down through Lough Beg to Newferry and past Portglenone from January through till April. Though vast, the shoals do not fill the entire river; some obviously migrate from Lough Neagh, some from Lough Beg, and no doubt there are resident shoals too, thus to maximise the potential of locations we split up into two groups. Terry and Ray would try below the bridge at Toome in the deep water, while the remaining four of us tried the 'inform' length at New Ferry where local anglers have been regularly enjoying 50 lb plus catches, mainly consisting of big hybrids.

For both fishing and photography we could not have picked a better day. The river was pulling through nicely with a good colour and the depth just beyond a ten metre pole line was over 12 feet. We made up quiver tip rods and cage feeder rigs for a method change, but the swims right beside the adjacent car park, where the local council has provided amenities to attract visiting anglers, were simply screaming out to be pole fished. Kevin sorted me out a 10 g float rig (I'm always scrounging his rigs) and after putting in a dozen caster and maggot filled balls of stodge, I was into a chunky hybrid on the very first pull through, after setting the float so that the bait just held back off the bottom. Such is the size and

The enormous River Bann system in Northern Ireland offers superlative freshwater sport even during the coldest winter months. This is due to the vast shoals of roach, bream and hybrids which migrate from Lough Neagh and Beg into the Bann at Toome Bridge, Newferry and Portglenone. Here I heave my Avon quiver tip rod into a jumbo hybrid at Newferry during a research trip for Go Fishing.

The deep waters of the River Bann at Newferry, which vary between 12 and 16 feet close into the bank, permit huge hybrids to be caught on the pole.

Kevin Ashurst is better known as an international match fisherman and former world champion but he gets amongst the big bream too – like this 7 lb beauty.

fighting capacity of these massive hybrids between 1½ and 3½ lb, that fishing with anything less than a 4 lb bottom and size 14 hook is asking for trouble. In the end I went down to a ten holding five maggots, and they still swallowed it up.

I was as excited as a kid with a new toy. Though I regularly fished the Lea and Thames with an old Sowerbutts bamboo pole during my youth, today's 10–12 m carbon poles call for a completely different technique, or your arm falls off in next to no time. The secret lies in steadying the butt end under the crutch against the seat, while supporting its length two feet along with the right hand. You 'lift' steadily into a bite, rather than strike, and when hooked up onto a good fish the sensation is entirely different to all other methods.

As the day wore on the wind increased to almost gale force, making the pressure against an 11 m pole when vertical and bringing a fish to the net, tremendous. Suddenly from the next peg downstream there was a loud 'crack', followed by laughter from both sides as the top three joints of John Roberts' pole snapped off like a carrot and followed his float into the Bann. There is no sympathy fishing with these guys, believe me.

The entire section of the river for a good 100 yards seemed to be crammed full with quality roach to over the pound and unusually large hybrids. There is certainly nowhere in the British Isles, and possibly the whole of Europe, where hybrids grow so large and are to be found in such enormous numbers. By two o'clock in the afternoon the light was perfect for a bag shot, so Martin did the honours with the Nikon while Kevin, John and I hauled our nets out. Well over 200 lb between the three of us in less than five hours was, I am certain, nothing out of the ordinary for this river. Dozens and dozens of the hybrids topped 3½ lb, more than I had ever seen in over 30 years of serious fishing. Once these fish had been carefully returned we carried on for another hour, now on the feeder since the gale force winds made pole fishing impossible, and we continued to catch. In retrospect, I feel the feeder would probably have been a faster method with these big hybrids in such conditions. On our way back to the hotel we picked up Terry and Ray who had accounted for just five roach between them fishing a variety of swims below Toome. We had no doubts as to where we would all be fishing on the second day.

After yesterday heavy overnight snow would have seemed impossible, yet as we heartily tucked into a typical Irish breakfast, huge snow flakes gusted along the main road outside the hotel. With at least a 10° overnight drop in temperature accompanied by a swirling blizzard, and with so much snow water in the river, we were far from optimistic about prospects and in no hurry to begin the day's sport. For the first couple of hours our fears were confirmed, it was as though there wasn't a single fish in the very stretch of water which had yesterday treated us so generously. By midday however, those lovely big hybrids started moving over the groundbait and on feeder rigs with the bait static we

24 Wednesday

Overcast with occasional patches of sun following heavy overnight snow. Freezing cold north-westerly wind.

all started slowly to catch, although the bites were tentative and spasmodic. Terry Smith and Ray Bows eventually managed to draw a haul of roach and hybrids close in over their ten metre pole line and took fish by running the bait through very slowly. Holding the quiver tip rod was enough for me, and I started to remember the immortal voice of Fred J. Taylor saying: 'I'll be glad when I've had enough of this' – a more quintessential phrase has yet to be created for the fisherman. Kevin Ashurst banged into the only bream caught during the two days, a really thick-set beauty of between 6–7 lb, while Terry Smith put a memorable second day's net together by consistent work with the pole. Over 80 lb of quality hybrids and roach in such adverse conditions was nothing less than amazing.

During the afternoon, simply taking the photographs was enough for hands which I could barely feel, whilst Martin and John Roberts sat in Kevin's estate with the heater on full blast before eventually succumbing to the warmth of the bar and its Guinness back at the Hotel. Strange really that those fish should have fed on, I imagine that because there are so many hybrids per shoal, there is always an element of competition which keeps them biting. I could not have expected so much as a sucked maggot from my local Norfolk rivers in identical conditions, but that's the beauty of Ireland's River Bann and what makes it such an attractive winter venue.

As we were not due to leave Northern Ireland till late on Thursday afternoon, Martin (who loves making out itineraries on his word processor) had planned a tour into the Sperrin Mountains so that I could investigate a few trout streams for possible programme material. But all this was quickly abandoned early Thursday morning with the news that the Liverpool car ferry had broken down. This meant a drive to Larne for Martin and the boys to catch the ferry over to Stranraer in Scotland, followed by a 250 mile drive back south into Yorkshire. All the time the weather was worsening to gale force winds. Before setting off for Larne they rushed me over to Belfast Airport to catch an earlier plane. As it turned out, they all arrived home 24 hours later even then, because their ferry had to lay off Stranraer for several hours in rough seas, unable to dock. The plane flight into Heathrow in lashing rain and violent winds, was not much smoother. Even the pilot

The Bann is so prolific in jumbo hybrids to over 4 lb (not to mention quality roach) that Terry Smith, master rod builder from Sheffield, accounted for this 80 lb haul despite biting winds and heavy snow showers.

remarked that it was the hairiest flight he had ever made, coinciding with the strongest winds for over two years since the hurricane which devastated the south of England in 1988.

I had decided to stay overnight at my brother Dave's place in Cheshunt, Herts, a mere 30 mile drive along the M25 from Heathrow. But I hadn't bargained for the terrifying sight of dozens of tall sided lorries crashing over on their sides in the roaring winds. In addition to fallen trees, disintegrating road signs were being blown onto cars waiting in long jams whilst police and recovery gangs fought to clear the congestion. Five hours later I was very glad to be knocking on David's front door with the Saab still intact and fit for the drive back to Norwich in the morning. Who said that fishing is a relaxing sport?

Sunday 4

Overcast with sunny patches.
Strong, cold westerly breeze.

Joan and Chilli have run the Bridge Inn at Lenwade for over 30 years, so not surprisingly their farewell evening attracted most of the regulars in the village, eager to wish them well in retirement. Afterwards Jeff and Jane who run the mill opposite laid on a late night, or rather early morning, supper and so inevitably all my plans of rising early for once to enjoy a spot of roach fishing were dashed. When I did manage to reach the stream at 9.30 am it was only to find it way over the fields as a result of the previous two days of torrential rain, far higher than I had anticipated. At least Norfolk was enjoying some badly needed rain after almost a year of exceedingly low water tables, not that this was going to help me put some nice roach on the bank.

Walking along a ridge of high ground adjacent to the stream where it exits from the lake in a wide waterfall, I settled into a nice-looking swim with slack water a little downstream on the inside of the bend, bordered along the margins by a thick mat of sweet rush. Offering a completely static bait was the order of the day in the cold, orange-coloured water, so I chose a block end feeder rig holding a mixture of maggots and casters, and sat back to concentrate on the quiver tip with three maggots on a size 16 presented close alongside the rushes. Three hours later and having tried half a dozen such swims, I felt that after missing one clonking bite and a couple of twitches it was time to head back to the car. Stupidly I had put on wellies instead of thermal boots and my feet were nearly frozen off.

Nice to get the first blank of the year out of the way.

Wednesday 7

Heavily overcast, lashing rain.
Gale force south-westerly wind.

For two consecutive winters now, snowdrops have poked through in January and been in full bloom by early February, covering the mossy gaps between the line of great oaks and beech from the lodge to the stream in a cloak of white velvet. Is this due to genuine changes in our climate or simply coincidence? Global warming however could not have been further from our minds as brother Dave and I unloaded the car. What a day we had picked to sample the delights of stream fishing! A gale force south-westerly was blowing,

In torrential rain, accompanied by cold gale-force winds and with the stream bankhigh and full of leaves, brother David and I would have settled for the odd bite apiece. Yet out came this superb roach pushing the magical 2 lb mark.

Through careful feeding by packing bronze maggots into a blockend and ledgering close into the bank, the big roach was joined in the net by two more, plus a brace of perch. All accepted three maggots on a size 16 hook.

accompanied throughout the day by torrential rain. On the assumption that the little stream I had fished on Sunday would be back within its banks and nicely fishable, Dave had driven up from the outskirts of London to Norfolk, bent on enjoying my prediction of the roach feeding in earnest. It really would all have been on the cards if only the narrow stream had carried a little less floodwater and fewer leaves. In fact I had got it wrong and at least another two days without rain were needed, but we were there and had to make the best of it.

As the flow was still fairly pushing through, I fancied our best chance was quiver tipping using a small block end feeder to trickle a line of maggots alongside the mat of sweet reed grass. Initial casts produced an eel apiece, which illustrated the unseasonal mildness of the air temperature, though the cutting wind and rain belied this, followed by a nice roach for me pushing the 2 lb mark. This immediately fired Dave's enthusiasm, especially when another roach of about a pound grabbed hold on the very next cast. This excitement was rather short-lived, because we then had to wait a good two hours for another series of bites, which again fell to my rod following several moves both up and down the short length. The roach were there alright – I kept assuring Dave that they couldn't possibly all have jumped out onto the bank – but nothing so much as a sucked maggot came his way, until the tip was suddenly wrenched round, and he promptly broke on the strike. Words could not describe the look on his face.

I would love to report that during the last hour those roach came on and Dave got well in amongst the two pounders for which the stream is renowned. Alas, conditions actually worsened. The level rose, the water became even muddier and by 3.30 pm we had had more than enough, feeling and looking to all intents and purposes like the proverbial pair of drowned rats.

I added a smaller roach and two 12 oz perch to the catch, all on three maggots on a size 16, but it was scant reward for several hours of concentration in such appalling conditions. Dave and I agreed that it was one of the worst days we had ever endured. Perhaps next week when I travel down to fish with him on the Kennet near Newbury, mother nature won't be in such a foul mood.

Steve Allen, who had been badgering me to take him chub fishing for longer than I care to remember, arrived at the back door as dawn broke accompanied by the kind of conditions that make you wish you had stayed in bed. Not the best chances of extracting chub from an unsettled River Wensum I mused, as I put the coffee on and finished the remains of the washing-up from the night before. It had been a late bash with good company and liberal helpings of chilli, garlic bread and red wine. Surprisingly I actually felt in better shape than three hours of sleep would suggest.

11 Sunday

Clear sky at dawn followed by heavy cloud cover for remainder of day. Strong, bitterly cold north-westerly wind.

The morning after a late night bash I would have preferred a lie-in, but Steve Allen had been promised a chubbing session. From the River Wensum at Taverham he took beauties to 3½ lb on quiver tipped breadflake.

With the wind fairly buffeting the car along the Fakenham Road we stopped at Taverham Road Bridge to see the state of the Wensum, and hey presto, without rain for the last two days, the gravel bottom could be seen through a foot of water. Chub fishing was not now just a possibility, but a sure thing, though Steve had no doubt heard such confident predictions before. After parking the car in the farmyard, we walked down the steep hill to the double 'S' bend, bordered on the opposite bank by tall poplars, now completely leafless and swaying violently. A classic chub lie if ever there was one. Having made up a batch of mashed bread from two old loaves the previous evening (makes your hands freezing cold if done at the river), several golf balls were squeezed out and lobbed upstream about a third of the way out. Our first position was on the inside of a left swinging bend, immediately up from a long straight into which the chub could move, followed by us, after taking a few from the bend itself. This is more or less exactly what happened.

I took five chub of between 2½–3½ lb in quick succession, all on quiver tipped breadflake on a three swan shot fixed pater-noster, holding a size 10 hook tied direct to the 5 lb reel line. Steve produced a lone, mint-condition roach of close on the pound, but initially found interpreting every movement of the quiver tip confusing. I suspect he did in fact miss several 'drop back' bites, thinking it was merely the ledger resettling, but eventually he got the hang of it.

When we moved a few yards around the bend, for a good hour or so we experienced bite after bite from what could only have been immature roach. Frustrating bites they were, being tiny plucks and rustles on the tip, most of which looked hittable but proved to the contrary. Every so often a typical chub bite would emerge and we both took one apiece and lost another. The eventual tally for this four hour morning stint added up to seven chub and one roach, which in the gusty, chilly conditions was certainly more than Steve had expected. The presence of such a large shoal of young roach was particularly interesting considering the Wensum's lack of sizeable shoals during recent years. I shall keep a watchful eye on this part of the river.

My long-time fishing pal, Doug Allen from Norwich, weighs what every river angler dreams of – a 2 lb plus roach.

This morning might easily have materialised into one of the best roach sessions ever on the River Wensum, if I had not needed to pack up at 8 am to open the shop in Norwich an hour later. Talk about frustration.

It began while it was still black outside with Doug Allen's car crunching down the gravel lane and starting the dogs barking. Years of roach fishing has taught us the importance of light values and of that first hour after dawn has broken, so we enjoyed a rushed cuppa and made the short drive to the local weir pool. Doug chose to ledger the deep swirling waters of the main pool, while on a hunch based on a nice catch of roach up to 2½ lb from the straight immediately above the weir at this time last year, I opted for a light waggler rig and a spell of long trotting using two bronze maggots on a size 16 tied direct to the 2 lb reel line. If anything, the upper river was low, and pulling through rather too fast in my opinion. Obviously I was wrong, because on the second trot down the peacock waggler sank positively and in came a deep-bodied

14 Wednesday

Very mild. Overcast, with spasmodic patches of sunshine. Moderate south-westerly wind.

Above: Dave Wilson catches a pound chub from a small pool on trotted maggots, only to have it cough up a lamprey into his hand.

Above right: River keeper David Culley displays the size of dace for which Royal Berkshire's Kennet is justly famous – almost a pound.

roach of around 10 oz. This was repeated on the following cast, and the next and so on. All beautifully conditioned fish, absolutely scale perfect. After returning a dozen or so, they were coming so thick and fast that I decided to retain a few of the larger specimens for the camera. Exactly one hour later when time forced me to pack up, the keepnet contained a good baker's dozen of silver-sided beauties between 1½ and 1¾ lb. And those roach were still biting! Meanwhile, Doug had caught on a feeder rig presenting double maggot on a size 14, a large grayling and two roach. One of 6 oz, the other pulling the dial scales down to 2 lb 1 oz. What fantastic sport the mild conditions had allowed us to enjoy, in less than one and a half hours' fishing.

Reluctantly, after capturing the occasion with the camera, I pointed the Saab towards Norwich leaving a contented Doug to enjoy the rest of the day ledgering the pool, where he went on to catch another 20 roach up to 1½ lb, several perch to the pound, and a surprise 3 lb tench. I would have loved to share the rest of the day with him. As it was, by 9.15 am I was selling maggots to other fishermen.

The two Davids make the best of a flooded valley with quiver tipped maggots presented close into the bank, accounting for chub, huge dace and out-of-season trout.

Beggars can't be choosers, but Wilson would rather have caught this huge grayling of almost 2 lb long-trotting instead of blockend feedering.

Thursday 15

*Bright sky all day long.
Cold westerly wind.*

I seem to be driving rather regularly down south from Norwich these days to fish with brother Dave. In fact we have fished more together in the weeks since my wife and I separated just before Christmas, than during the last 20 years. One of the advantages of being single again, though perhaps Dave's wife Lyn would argue with that.

Our destination was the lovely River Kennet above Newbury where we had fished a few weeks back. This necessitated a six o'clock start from Cheshunt to hit the dreaded M25 and then the M4, before the rush hour traffic became impossible. Through not paying attention (gassing too much) we followed the wrong signs and found ourselves taking a quick tour of Heathrow Airport, Terminal 3 to be precise. Dave was not amused by my hysterics, as he sped around looking for the way out. Nevertheless, despite a breakfast stop in Newbury, we arrived on David Culley's doorstep promptly at 8 am, only to see the river still brimming full to the banks with floodwater. That old saying 'February fill dyke' could not have been more apt. This was not exactly a welcome sight to the ardent grayling fisherman. In complete contrast to dace, roach and chub, grayling rarely feed with enthusiasm in heavily coloured water, so it looked as though a decidedly patchy day lay ahead.

After a quick cuppa we followed the tiny sluice stream through flooded meadows to a lovely little pool, and here, showing a liking for Dave's trotted maggots, were dace, a couple of spotties and a small chub of around 12 oz which promptly coughed up a partly digested brook lamprey. Having already grabbed a substantial mouthful, this greedy beggar still managed to suck in Dave's bunch of maggots on a size 14. After this diversion we headed towards the main river where we decided to knuckle down and search out some of the slacks close in to the bank with quiver tip and block end feeder. Strangely, for all the river's height, the actual colour was not that thick (a visibility of around 12″), and I fancy that had it not been for bright sunshine coupled to an extremely chilly wind blowing down the valley from west to east, a few nice roach would have shown. As it was, our ledgered maggots were fair game for the aggressive rainbows, which invariably appeared on either the first or second cast in every swim, before things settled down and the dace started to come. And what dace they were too. Long, deep in the belly and thick across the shoulders, with a few individuals nudging the 15 oz mark. From a six foot deep slack immediately below the sharp bend I took on successive casts, a dace of 14 oz followed by a grayling of just under 2 lb, my best ever from the Kennet. I would have rather taken it long trotting. Somehow, grayling caught ledgering just do not have the same appeal.

Brother Dave must have given just about every fishable hole and slack on the main river a try, not to mention all the carrier's pools, taking numerous quality dace plus the odd small chub. But those roach refused to feed, even during the so-called 'magical' hour leading into darkness when we thought it would all happen. Our feet simply got colder and that was it. I felt particularly sorry for our host David Culley, who fell over up to his waist in a flooded ditch late in the

Conditions really do make all the difference between poor and memorable sport. With the stream at last in superb winter trim, Andy Jubb nets a fine roach.

To the untrained eye this 2 lb fish looks like a roach. It is, in fact, a superbly conditioned roach/rudd hybrid caught on long-trotted maggots by Andy.

afternoon, only to return from the house with a new set of dry clothes on, to find he'd put on a perished pair of boots with holes in both feet. We were not sorry to pack up.

Sunday 18

*Much milder with sunny periods.
Moderate, westerly winds.*

With all the long-distance driving I have done of late, I fancied a few hours roaching on a local water, and as I had promised Andy Jubb (who manages my tackle shop) a session before making the annual pilgrimage to India and its mahseer next Saturday, we visited the little stream where brother Dave and I fished two weeks back when it was in full flood. This time however (there is always an excuse, isn't there), we could have done with being a few days earlier because the stream was now back to normal level with little colour. This necessitated 3BB waggler rigs, 2 lb main line and a size 20 hook to a 1½ lb bottom. Bait varied from maggot to casters and back to maggot again, with double bronze maggot scoring most effectively. We tried several swims on both sides of the narrow course and needed to long trot a good 20 yards to instigate bites through the middle channel which averaged around three feet deep.

Despite a sizeable pike lunging on the surface at the first roach of the day as I slid the net out over the marginal rushes (fortunately it never put in a repeat performance), Andy and I caught slowly but steadily for most of the morning. By lunchtime however, bites became non-existent due to the bright sunlight and ridiculously clear water. But we had planned to finish by then anyway. Best fish was Andy's roach/rudd hybrid of around the two pounds mark; all the rest were quality roach from 12 oz up to 1¾ lb, many covered in black spot, a parasite infecting the scales but which rarely seems to affect growth rates. These roach were deep and as fat as butter with that lovely blue-silver sheen across the back which only winter river roach have. What a lovely morning – extremely mild with daffodils and crocuses in full bloom (in the middle of February) and roach on the centre-pin trotting. Could a fisherman ask for more?

INDIAN INTERLUDE

2 3 February

An hour after dawn and as usual the dogs were impatient for their walk around the lakes. For me the morning was rather special as it afforded me my last, long look at Norfolk in February before setting off for the warmth, the perfumes, the friendships and the huge freshwater fish of India. This is a pilgrimage that Andy Davison and I have made for the last three years. During January and February of 1985, 1986 and 1987 my two lakes froze over and remained solid for several weeks. Some of the lowest temperatures in living memory were recorded at this time, and in January 1987 the family was actually housebound for five days, unable to drive through the height of snow covering the narrow lane from the house onto the main Fakenham Road. That's the price you pay for living in seclusion. It is rather a contrast that as I write we are enjoying the century's hottest ever February. However the fact that I will miss out on a potentially bumper end to the coarse fishing season does not bother me one bit.

Spending an entire fishing trip in the company of just one person means that he needs to be one hell of a good friend. Indeed, except for my brother Dave, I cannot think of another mate whose long-term company I would wish to share other than Andy's.

Hostile is the only way of describing the river valley, which is why few bother to make the long, dusty journey by jeep over boulder strewn tracks in order simply to fish. In addition to the sickening heat which rises to over 100 degrees at midday, there are wild elephants and snakes to be wary of at night. Yet the thought of hooking into a leviathan mahseer brings us back time and time again.

This year' trip has already taken on a new format with the addition of Andy's girlfriend Julie. It's a situation that Andy was not happy about initially, I insisted that if Julie really wanted to come, she should do so, and finally he agreed. Besides, the presence of a woman in the camp has a civilising influence on the all-male fishing holiday, which I for one appreciate.

The flight, lasting eight hours from Heathrow to Delhi and then on to Bombay went as smoothly as usual, thanks to Martin Founds who had booked us in club class. In contrast to previous trips we managed to pass straight through Bombay customs hall without unpacking a thing, and promptly caught a taxi to the domestic airport for the penultimate leg of our journey, a two hour flight in an air bus. With the addition of five hours to the clock, this brought the local time to 8.30 Sunday morning. We were met at the airport by Susheel's driver who showed us the easy way out of the city and then caught a bus back to the house, leaving Andy (can't keep him away from the wheel) the arduous four hour drive down to the river.

We met Susheel and his lovely wife Nanda three summers ago on our first mahseer expedition and they have been firm friends ever since. Susheel even extends his hospitality into lending us a jeep for the duration of our stay, without which we could never get to explore the river valley so thoroughly, the terrain being hostile, to say the least. Walking any more than a mile or two over rocks interspersed with thorn scrub in temperatures of over 100° saps the strength unbelievably quickly; we have suffered sun stroke and dehydration on several occasions and have now learnt not to court danger.

Seeing the river again was a wonderful moment. Vultures and fish eagles were nesting in the tall mutti and tamarind trees above the campsite and brahminy and pirah kites cruised the thermals high above the valley, mobbed by dusky and river terns if they invaded their territory. Along the edge of the flood plain, nourished annually from June until August by the monsoon rains, the trees were bright green, indicating that the monsoon had been higher and had probably lasted longer than last year's. We would no doubt be treated each morning to the sights of samba, spotted deer, wild boar, jackals and elephants coming to drink from the river.

In addition to the prolific wildlife, Andy and I have in the last three years come to love the beautiful flowers, the colours, the perfumes and above all the friendliness of the people. Even the harshness of India, which is at first so shocking, has become a vital part of the experience. Last but not least of course is the very creature we come back year after year to do battle with. The most ledgendary, exciting and enigmatic of tropical river fish, talked about all over the world, yet caught by comparatively few: the mahseer. Inhabiting the strongest currents in the fastest, most boulder-strewn parts of the river, it feeds on a diet largely consisting of freshwater crabs and other fishes. The mahseer is a giant carp/barbel-like creature capable of reaching 150 lb. It possesses enormous fins and scales, with long barbules hanging from its cavernous, toothless mouth. Situated in the throat however, are powerful pharyngeal teeth used for crunching food to pulp. The pharyngeals of a 70 lb mahseer for instance would be as large as a young man's hand.

We ended the long drive over rocky tracks to where Susheel and Nanda were camped beside the river at Crocodile Pool (yes there are crocs in the river too), with around two hours of daylight remaining. It was, as always, an emotional meeting with hugs all round, and it was great to see our two guides again, Suban and Bola. They are both friends and teachers, who have given us so much of their river knowledge, we could never begin to repay them.

Talk quickly got around to current prospects; apparently sport had been rather slow prior to our arrival and Suban attributed the mahseer's reluctance to feed to low water temperatures which of course slow down the metabolic rate of any fish. When sport was really humming last year for instance, the river was running at an incredible 87°. Now, after weeks of unusually cold weather (well, cold for India that is), and heavy flooding resulting from an irrigation dam being opened some 100 miles up river for a period of six days, water temperatures were only just touching 70°. However, as the day-time temperatures were steadily increasing, with an ever dropping water level, we were optimistic that it would all come together in a few days. On Monday we took things slowly, trying all the known pools and runs but without much joy. Andy took two baby mahseer of 2 lb and 5 lb on ragi paste from a deep pool about one mile below the camp, and I missed one good bite. But it was enough to be back dressed in just a pair of shorts and feeling the warmth of the sun while watching pied kingfishers hover above the surface.

In technical terms mahseer fishing is rather like ledgering for giant barbel, which of course is what they are, as their latin name 'barbus tor' suggests. The rod is always held, lest it gets pulled in, and the reel (we use 9,000 and 10,000 ABU multipliers) is kept in free spool held with the thumb. This

Right: John's guide Suban uses a castnet to gather small, bottom-feeding fish called chilwa from amongst the rock pools to use as dead baits for mahseer.

allows for several feet of line to be taken before clamping down, hitting hard, and slamming the reel into gear. When a big mahseer grabs the bait, the sensation is rather like the hook being suddenly connected to a lorry doing 30 miles an hour. When it narrows, the river is doing some 10 to 15 knots, hence the reason for our using a reel line of 40 lb test and 6/0 to 8/0 hooks. In a snag-free environment 20 lb line would perhaps be sufficient even to subdue a fish which regularly reaches 80 to 90 lb, but because of the danger of line shredding as big fish tear it across bedrock, there has to be a safety margin.

Though fresh crab, with which the bottom of the river is

full, would make an excellent natural bait for mahseer, it does not cast too well, so to combat the fast currents and the occasional necessity of long casting (70–90 yards) we use two baits consistently: chilwa, the name given to any small fish of between five and nine inches long, and ragi, a stiff paste made from millet flour which is boiled for 25 minutes to bring out the natural gluten and make it rubbery. This then withstands the constant pecking from small fish and remains on the hook for anything up to 20 minutes. Approximately 15″ above the hook some beaten lead strip is wound tightly around the line, the object of this is to encourage the lead to snag between the rocks and thus hold the bait where it is put. A mahseer then releases the lead strip in no uncertain terms with the most savage of bites.

27 Tuesday

This morning we made the long walk down to the rapids at the bottom of Crocodile Pool, where within half an hour Andy was fast into a big fish which instantly tore off downstream right between huge boulders in the middle of the river. Bola and Suban were quickly there risking life and limb untangling the line from the rocks in unbelievably fast currents – all to no avail. The hook had been shed. We were all gutted – losing the first big one hooked is always particularly depressing – and the walk back to camp seemed so much longer.

After our siesta (it is too hot to do anything in the heat of the day) I made up a light float rig with a size 10 hook and caught some chilwa (small carnatic carp) on breadflake – what a universal bait bread is. These went into a bucket and off we set in two coracles down the first rapids towards a favourite lie called centre rock. Some 50 yards below the black protrusion, just large enough to sit three, there is a crop of subsurface rocks with a huge boil of ruffled water behind. This is a classic mahseer lie. Julie, Suban and I fished together while Andy and Bola perched on a similar rock almost opposite so that we could all present baits down the same long run and help each other with photographing

Facing: While kites, eagles and vultures are everyday sights along the river valley, owls are not. Yet this young owl loved being photographed.

whoever got stuck in first. We needed the coracle to get to this run and it becomes even more vital if a big fish takes off downstream into lower pools and you need to follow it. This is exactly what happened. After missing a strong hit on chilwa, no sooner had I recast almost to the same area just behind the rocks, when over went the rod, and the line fairly sizzled beneath my thumb. The sudden shock of slamming the reel into gear seemed to send the fish berserk, because it rocketed off down the pool taking 50, 75 then over 100 yards. The spool was now emptying fast so Suban and I gave chase in the coracle leaving poor Julie alone on the rock. At the end of the pool the water diverts into several mini pools between enormous protruding rocks, it was here that the mahseer had gone to ground. The line was so entangled that Suban grounded the coracle on a shallow ledge and swum out to free it. As the line clipped over the last rock the fish, which was thankfully still attached, pulled so hard that the coracle started to drift off the ledge towards the next set of rapids with Suban 20 feet away. Had I not frantically grabbed and managed to hold on with my left hand leaning half out of the coracle, I don't like to think what might have happened. Anyhow Suban was soon back on the paddle and off we shot down into the next pool.

Andy and I have an unwritten law that whenever one of us hooks up on something big, the other guy gets on the camera as fast as he can – and sure enough Bola and Andy, who I hadn't time to notice up till now, came alongside to help and to get the best shots. This pool was the last before the main rapids and it was all or nothing; not even Suban would risk going down a five foot drop into boulders the size of a car with a big fish on, so I started to really give it some welly. What I didn't like however, was a clump of shredded line stuck in the tip ring. After another 15 minutes it suddenly came to the surface in an almighty boil – 'beeg feesh sir' said Suban – and as usual he was right. The angler can take heart when a mahseer surfaces because it means the battle can be won, and since this was the first time in 45 minutes that we had set eyes upon our adversary we felt elated. Several heavy but short runs later, there it was up on the surface, totally exhausted. Suban jumped into the water to thread a stringer through its gills; landing nets and keepnets are totally useless for this kind of fishing. A soft cord threaded through the gills and tied in a big loop allows the mahseer to swim back out into the fast water and get its badly needed breath back. After a ten minute rest we allowed the current to deposit us on the sandy beach at the far side of the pool where the scales and giant sling were made ready. Bola went 300 yards back upstream in

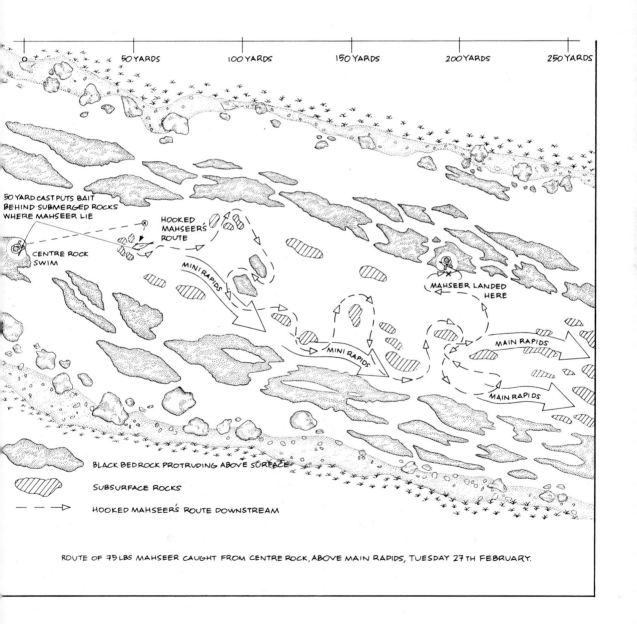

ROUTE OF 75 LBS MAHSEER CAUGHT FROM CENTRE ROCK, ABOVE MAIN RAPIDS, TUESDAY 27TH FEBRUARY.

Facing, top: Andy and Bola came alongside in the second coracle to help and to obtain the best shots while the giant mahseer held station amongst the rocks of the last pool before the main rapids.

Facing, below: After a spectacular fight lasting almost an hour through pools and rapids over a distance of nearly 300 yards, Bola hoists John's 75 lb golden mahseer into the weigh sling.

the coracle to where I first hooked the monster to collect Julie, and when they, returned the mahseer was weighed. Bola had said 75 lb before it even went in the sling, and he was spot on. What a beauty, and what a great first fish with which to start the holiday. I have taken several larger, up to 92 lb in fact, but few fights have been so spectacular.

The fish was still a bit whacked after such a hard fight, so I stood chest-deep holding it against the current for a few minutes while the others, with daylight now starting to go, waded downstream to the end pool just above the rapids. Immediately Andy got fast into a big fish on chilwa which shot over the rapids snagging the line through a cluster of rocks in midstream. Suban was quick off the mark in rowing across the pool, and with a spare rod flipped the line over onto Andy's side of the rocks, enabling him to follow the mahseer down the rapids through the maze of huge boulders and white water. My fish was by now fully recovered and ready to be released – it's always a lovely sight to see them swim off strongly – so I grabbed the waterproof Nikon compact and stumbled through the rocky gullies towards the action. The mahseer had travelled fully 150 yards by now and gone to ground in a deep, swirling hole. Andy put on as much pressure as he dare, but he too was blighted by yards of frayed and shredded line, on the wrong side of the rod tip. This however was one of those evenings to cherish, and everything ended happily. The mahseer eventually tired and after a good half hour fight an elated Andy finally drew his prize through the white water into Bola's arms. Not as big as we had all thought, but then such a fight could have come from any mahseer in the 50–80 lb bracket. As it was, Andy's fish lumped the scales down to 60 lb exactly. What a spectacular session!

As is customary following a great catch (and two such mahseer within an hour of each other is nothing less than incredible), everybody drank well that evening from what has become our special 'mahseer punch'. It is concocted from the juice of six fresh limes, a large water melon, half a bottle of gin, half a bottle of dark rum, lemon squash, the milk from several coconuts plus water to top up, on a five to one ratio against the spirits. Well, roughly anyway. The only drawback is that when you wake up bleary eyed the following morning

to the irrepressible sound of crickets ringing in your ears, and reach for the toilet bag crammed full of items for every eventuality, one large tube seems very much like another. That's when you find that brushing your teeth with germolene is not very pleasant. Serves me right!

Thursday 1

Yesterday passed very slowly in fishing terms, despite a long drive downstream through thorn scrub tracks to our favourite gorge where the entire river condenses to just 20 yards wide. From this incredibly fast, swirling section which we call the 'narrows' where depth averages over 20 feet, we have in past years taken several leviathan golden mahseer between 70 and 95 lb.

This morning we tried again and hey presto Andy took a ten pounder straight away on chilwa. Then at around 10.30 am when we are usually thinking about stopping fishing due to the intense heat and the strength of the sun's rays, Andy belted into a good one, again on chilwa, which went straight down some narrow rapids. Mahseer are not silly – this necessitated a swim across the river, and Bola and Suban helped Andy while I trooped behind snapping away with our two waterproof Nikons. Eventually the mahseer tired just downstream of a house-sized rock in the middle of the rapids, onto which Andy needed to climb in order to apply maximum pressure. After a 40 minute tussle the result was a lovely long golden mahseer of 52 lb.

Upon returning to our camp at lunchtime, the excitement started. Bola and Suban suddenly went running off down towards the rapids where several loud explosions meant only one thing: poachers were dynamiting the river. Andy, Julie and I followed on with the cameras as the guides like photos of the poachers holding their plunder for police evidence. We arrived just in time to see two guys high-tailing it across the shallows in mid-river – it looked like they might even get away. However, they had not accounted for Chick Raju our camp guard, who came in pursuit like someone out of a John Wayne movie, down the river in one of the coracles, easily catching the trailing poacher.

Facing top: Spotted deer graze peacefully on the edge of the jungle within the Nagaraholi wild-life park, free from poachers and tigers.

Facing below: Against all odds, the line almost shredded to nothing by rocks, the 60 lb mahseer is finally extracted from the rapids and drawn into Bola's arms.

Bola located the poachers' fish, two small mahseer, two pink carp, a carnatic carp and two black carp (about 10 lb in all) and their clothes which contained the keys to a motorbike hidden close to the river track. Andy walked back to camp to fetch the jeep and pick everyone up, including the poacher, while I rode the bike back. It was not the easiest of rides along rocky elephant tracks believe me. As I write this, the forlorn young poacher sits not three yards away with tears in his eyes, staring out across the water and black rocks, no doubt pondering his plight. The guides will hand him over to Susheel when he returns tomorrow evening and then, possibly, the police.

In the evening we fished the long pool upstream of the camp where I missed just one hit on ragi paste. For the record, evening air temperature back in camp at 10 pm was 91°, while the water temperature was exactly 80°.

Friday 2

It is now Friday morning at 11 am and the air temperature is just over 100°. If the thermometer is laid on my tackle bag or on the rocks the mercury rises to between 120°–130°. We fished the central rock area of the rapids again and I bagged two baby mahseer of 5 and 10 lb on chilwa and also missed another take.

Four o'clock is our usual afternoon starting time for mahseer, just as the sun is beginning to lose its intensity. We used the coracles to explore the first rapids close to camp, Andy and Julie trying the upper pools with Bola, while Suban and I drifted down to the last two pools immediately above the main rapids. After missing a clonking hit on chilwa accompanied by Suban's usual scolding, old-fashioned look, I managed to redeem myself by catching a lovely, incredibly long and comparatively sleek fish of just over 40 lb. Had the hook pulled, we would have guessed its weight as double. The light was now going rapidly, leaving just enough time for one last cast into the pool above the main rapids where our last chilwa produced a small, unusually coloured mahseer of 10 lb. It was dark on the back with silver fins and a greenish body; Suban called it a 'green' mahseer. There are in fact several colour mutations of what looks to be the same species, including golden (the most common), black, silver, red and now green; but so far no one has made a definitive study of all the variations.

Late in the evening after dinner, Susheel arrived and pointed out that if we took the poacher into the nearest town and police station, our planned trip up-river for tomorrow would be ruined. So, having spent two days away from his no doubt very worried family (punishment enough) and signing a letter admitting to his dynamiting exploits, he was off. The tinny sound of his four stroke engine vibrating through the trees and thorn sounds like an alien being, disturbing for many minutes the special quietness we have come to love about the valley. This beautiful place is usually free from sounds of the modern world, and I hope it will always remain that way. This very special part of India with its wonderful wildlife and rich river valley remains a microcosm of what all river valleys in India were once like. Unfortunately, as a result of over-exploitation and indiscriminate poaching, netting and dynamiting, most Indian rivers are mere ghosts of their former glory, when mahseer were prolific throughout the system.

Though the following two days passed without a single mahseer being caught, we enjoyed an exploratory trip starting from a point way above the camp to a part of the river we had never previously seen, let alone fished. Breathtaking scenery and wonderful-looking mahseer rapids were reward enough. I hooked one modest fish of around 15 lb on ragi paste, which inexplicably came adrift after a couple of minutes, and that was that. But other experiences, such as disturbing a black bear interested by the food in our makeshift camp and finding dozens of plovers' nests on a huge island of bedrock in the middle of the river, made the trip wonderful all the same.

4 Sunday

Having arrived back at the camp we took a siesta till 4 pm and then went downstream to fish the fast runs just above the main rapids which so far have produced the bulk of our sport. After bouncing chilwa deadbaits through several snaggy, turbulent runs behind subsurface boulders, I banged into a spirited fish of 18 lb which went downstream so fast even against heavy clutch pressure, that we were forced to follow in pursuit with the coracle. After releasing this fish we found ourselves conveniently grounded on a large flat rock just beneath the surface which seemed an excellent platform to fish the next run downstream, a long turbulent strip of water. Susheel, my coracle partner, was soon into a large, glutenous yellow catfish of about 3 lb which simply sat on the bottom with the chilwa stuck in its throat, banging the rod tip every few seconds. This brought the time to around 6.30 pm when we usually finish so that the guides can walk the coracles back upstream along the edge to the camp (it's impossible to paddle them back), before darkness engulfs the valley. I can remember saying to Suban, 'just another five minutes' . . . when wham! The take was so violent it nearly pulled me out of the coracle. Down and down the mahseer went, eventually to lie doggo in the end pool just up from the main rapids where, with darkness imminent, I had no intention of allowing it to go. Suban deposited Susheel on the rocks where the others were all fishing on the opposite bank (less weight then in the coracle) and came back for me. We zoomed through the fast currents into the end pool, and from the high position where Suban landed me on the rocks I managed to bully the fish into a huge layby where it slogged away for a good five minutes, every so often nearly pulling me off the rocks with violent shaking of its head. Suban made sure he grabbed hold of its huge jaws at the first attempt, which was just as well for the hook fell out into his hand. What a strange shaped mahseer it was, with a pronounced humpy back and a short, narrow tail root it looked almost as though someone had cut a chunk out from the middle and stuck the two halves together again. Whenever I catch freshwater fish of this distinctive format back home I call them 'stumpies' which just about sums them up. This stumpie weighed exactly 62 lb and we were not sure whether to class it as a golden or a black mahseer. In colour it came about halfway between the two, with only the faintest orange in its tail, but with a dark cast to the side edges. All in all it was a terrific session.

Monday 5

Having been thrown in at the deep end by agreeing to accompany Andy on a mahseer trip and after missing several slamming bites, Julie finally comes to grips with a golden mahseer in the turbulent race immediately above the main rapids and plays it expertly under the watchful eye of Suban.

Rising a little earlier than usual to photograph a beautiful orange and red sunrise, of a kind that only India seems to provide, we then fished down the main rapids for a good half mile. Both Suban (using Julie's rod) and Andy hooked into really big mahseer, though sadly for a short time only as each fish managed to sever the 40 lb line on jagged rocks within minutes of the hooks going home. Highlight of the morning was Julie's first mahseer, which made us all extremely happy; it was a golden and weighed around 15 lb. It was caught on chilwa, which we are now using exclusively in preference to ragi paste, which the fish seem to associate with danger when the same areas are regularly fished – rather like carp back home. Now that Julie is getting the hang of first lowering the rod and then pumping the fish upstream against the strong currents, she is surely ready for a big one.

Nothing of note happened during the evening session, again spent in the rapids (could be a case of over-fishing there), until just after the evening meal at around 9 pm. Crashing and crunching could be heard in midriver, just downstream from the campsite. Immediately we suspected elephants crossing the river, and sure enough a family of 24 were slowly wading across, less than 100 yards away, with an enormous bull tusker bringing up the rear as they always do. I cannot remember seeing anything quite so exciting as watching these majestic creatures in the dark through binoculars. Light from the moon was enough to reflect and outline the bull elephant's enormous stems of ivory, the right tusk clearly twisted inwards towards the trunk, with the left one only half the length – a legacy perhaps of past battles. Throughout the night they circled the camp and every so often a blood curdling bellow was heard echoing through the trees.

Tuesday 6

We made the long, hot drive down to the narrow gorge, but came away with only two small mahseer to show for our efforts. The evening stint proved much more fruitful back at the rapids close to camp where Andy took a really thick-set golden mahseer of almost 60 lb, and I followed behind with a 15 pounder. Fishing the first mile or so down from camp is now really productive. Perhaps the shallow water is warmed up much quicker by the intense sun, because we are enjoying good hits on every session. The average river temperature is now in the middle 80°s.

With the line back-lit by the early morning sun, Andy fights a big mahseer from the coracle immediately downstream of crocodile rocks.

Having polished off two huge saucepans (no punch bowl) of our special mahseer brew, which last night contained at least one bottle each of rum and gin, we woke this morning very much the worse for wear. The plan was for Julie and I to join Suban in the coracle and shoot all the rapids to a big rock pool 1½ miles downstream, while Andy and Bola went in the jeep. This was so that the coracle could then be loaded onto the jeep for our return to camp.

Though we actually left much later than usual, each nursing the headache of all headaches, bites came straight away from our position on a long strip of jagged rocks protruding from the middle of the river with fast water on both sides. Julie unfortunately missed the first bite, a real slammer. Then, only minutes later, a screaming run woke me from a nodding stupor, the fish had sucked up ragi paste (couldn't catch any chilwa in the cast nets) and was moving quickly upstream, wrapping the line around several unseen rocks. After a short but most enjoyable, head-shaking fight Suban beached the coracle 100 yards upstream of where the fish was hooked so that I could step ashore, easing the fat prize into his waiting arms. It was a lovely golden which tipped the scales at 54 lb. Suddenly, my hangover had disappeared.

7 Wednesday

Having taken Andy and Bola over 200 yards down river, the great fish is finally beaten and brought back for weighing and the trophy shot, shared by Julie – 61 pounds of golden mahseer with scales as large as beer mats.

At 2 pm we left camp for a lengthy drive up country to view several wildlife parks at the invitation of Nanda and Susheel. The Nagaraholi Reserve was particuarly interesting, and it was lovely to see other parts of this fascinating country. In addition to the usual deer, jackals, elephants and peacocks, we saw the Indian bison, better known as gaur, at close quarters; an enormous creature, larger than a Friesian bull and with a heavy set of horns. We stayed overnight at Nagaraholi in one of the jungle lodges and then made the long drive to Mysore to have lunch with the famous Van Ingen brothers, whose family has run an international taxidermy business since the turn of the century. Dewett Van Ingen still holds the record for the heaviest mahseer ever caught on rod and line, a massive fish of 120 lb, and to look through their fascinating collection of trophies and skulls was like going back in time to an age when a man's hunting or fishing prowess was judged by the size and number of stuffed trophies hanging on the wall. Along one end of their vast show hall were huge wooden plaques covered in the pharyngeal teeth of all the mahseer mounted by the Van Ingens, with the corresponding weight of each specimen written inbetween. The teeth of the 120 lb record fish were the size of a man's two hands. Along the opposite wall in a floor to ceiling glass-fronted cupboard, were dozens of skulls, mostly from man-eating tigers and lions. Each pure white skull had its own grisly story to tell – in the case of a particular tiger's skull, the victim had turned out to be the killer; the tiger's brain had been pierced by the long sharp horns of the very beast it attacked.

Susheel and Nanda asked us whether we fancied accompanying them on a wild boar hunt which had been arranged for the weekend. Beaters and a head guide were provided and the chase would follow a remote part of the river valley bordered by eucalyptus plantations and thick woodlands. As Andy and Julie both regularly shoot, they were all for it, but I wasn't so sure. Then I thought about it for a while and reasoned that as I like eating bacon, chops and especially sweet and sour pork, which someone else has to kill for me, it would be hypocritical to chicken out. So off we went.

Wild boar hunting is not so very different from pheasant shooting, where beaters flush birds out, hopefully somewhere in the direction of the waiting guns. But unlike the pheasant, wild boar are highly intelligent creatures with incredible powers of smell, and they never seem to come out of the bush where you expect them to. They are also a very dangerous animal, able to run incredibly fast and charge unpredictably. Their curled tushes, up to six inches long, can rip a man's thigh to the bone, whilst their jaws could crunch through that same leg. Even with a rifle or twelve bore, 300 lb plus of charging wild boar bearing down upon you is, to say the least, hairy. Fortunately I never had to find out, the only boar shot was by Andy and this was distributed amongst the villagers. Herds of wild boar have actually become a menace to crops in many parts of India, where a family's entire food source can be decimated overnight. After the shoot we stayed with Susheel and Nanda, making the long drive back to the river valley the following morning.

12 Monday

We finally arrived back at camp around lunchtime, picking up Bola and Suban en route from their tiny village, about 10 miles away. They think nothing of walking this distance in the sickening heat, which is now well over 100° by 11 o'clock in the morning. For our evening stint we fished the lower rapids once the guides had caught a few chilwa in the cast net. Almost immediately I got into a small fish of 14 lb. This was followed by Andy hitting into something which shot straight over the main rapids. Julie and I were by now positioned on rocks so far upstream it would have been impossible to reach the action in time – we could only guess that it was a monster. Half an hour later when darkness started to fall the flashes in the distance from Andy's camera could clearly be seen, even if he, Bola and the fish couldn't.

Suddenly Julie was almost pulled off the rock where we sat, legs dangling in the warm water, as her rod arched over and the line evaporated from the reel. At last she was into a good one which took 20 minutes of sweat to bring back upstream against such a torrent of water below us. Julie played the fish incredibly well with a mixture of brute force and patience (sounds funny but true) and eventually the gleam of the fish's scales in the moonlight could be seen only a few yards downstream where the mahseer wallowed on its side in the shallows. Suban was on it like a hawk and shortly Julie was cradling her 35 lb trophy. For once she didn't have any trouble smiling for the camera.

Andy and Bola walked up from the end of the rapids just as Julie's fish was being returned, confirming that their fish, a golden, was indeed a monster – tipping the scales down to 73 lb. Understandably in such a force of white water and rocks, this had been his best ever fight. I wish the light had not been going and I could have been down there quick enough to capture the action.

Tuesday 13

Headaches all round again this morning, invariably the case after doing well with mahseer. We tried the same runs through the top rapids again with just small fish of 8 lb and 6 lb for Andy and myself, though I was at one stage actually connected to a real slow-moving 'lorry' (we call the bigger mahseer lorries because that's what they feel like

Today all mahseer are returned to the river to fight again, but it hasn't always been so. Look at this impressive collection of mahseer pharyngeal teeth displayed at Van Ingens, India's most famous taxidermists. Each set is marked with the weight of the mahseer from which they were taken.

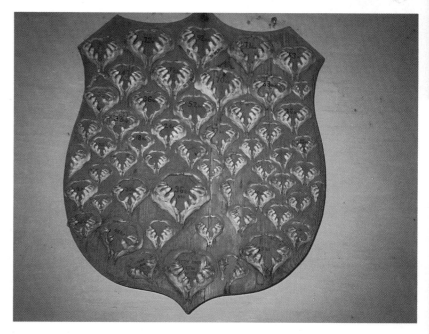

on the end) which moved progressively further down the long pool having snaffled up a large deadbait. For a good five minutes it seemed that this particular leviathan was not going to head for the rapids. Then, quite inexplicably, the 8/0 O'Shaunnessey fell out. Boy was I sick. In the afternoon session, Suban and I returned to the same stretch only two hundred yards upstream from my favourite centre rock position. And would you believe it, I promptly went and lost another lorry, the hook pulling after just 30 seconds. Once again I had to suffer an old-fashioned look from Suban.

Initially I wasn't so sure about going on a wild boar shoot, even though the animal does destroy huge areas of badly needed crops. But since I eat bacon and adore sweet and sour pork, playing the hypocrite wasn't on.

Wednesday 14

During the night a heavy storm and strong winds forced us all to take refuge in the tent instead of sleeping out in the open under the stars. In the morning we left camp early (for once) and drove down to crocodile rocks where I had taken the 54 pounder a few days back. This time it was Andy's turn, and he banged into a 61 pounder on the very first cast. Bola got the coracle ready as the fish sped off downstream at 20 miles an hour while I hastily connected the 300 mm lens onto the Nikon 301. Unfortunately I could only shoot into the early morning sun, but rattled off half a roll nevertheless.

As I sit penning this back in camp beneath the canopy of an enormous tamarind tree, we have just been treated to a wonderful sight. A brahminy kite has been circling a dead fish lying at the edge of the river – one of our discarded baits – not five yards from the table where breakfast is being served by Bala the camp boy. And now suddenly, it zooms in at incredible speed, talons fully extended, and grabs the fish so fast that our eyes are incapable of catching the moment. What a privilege to study so many birds of prey at close quarters; mahseer fishing is generous indeed.

Nothing to log during the evening session – a complete blank. On our return to camp we met Nanda who had arrived to spend the last two days' fishing with us, unfortunately without Susheel who couldn't get away from his office.

Thursday 15

Woke early and made the walk down river to try a couple of long shallow pools two miles below the main rapids. For a bit of competitive fun we matched the A Team – Nanda, Suban and myself – against the B Team – Andy, Julie and Bola. B Team swam across the river to fish the tempting mini rapids and pool feeding off the opposite bank, while the A Team presented chilwa deadbaits behind all the largest rocks in the middle of the river – both choice lies for the biggest mahseer. Within an hour I had managed to botch two lorry takes, on each occasion the hook point had reversed back into the bait. What a rotten run of luck. Nanda meanwhile was going great guns, taking a yellow cat of about 2 lb followed by a golden mahseer of 41 lb which put up an incredible scrap in the fast churning water. We tried one more pool on the walk back to camp where Nanda got fast into another lorry on the first throw across the turbulent run. Fortunately the mahseer hung in the current just shaking its head and swam slowly upstream. Had it gone down, we would have been in a right pickle without the coracle. Slowly the great fish, now visible in the clearing water, was drawn reluctantly against the strong flow – at least 10 knots of white water and boulders where a man would find it impossible to keep his footing. The mahseer rolled on the surface behind a large boulder and we all gasped – it was enormous, somewhere between 80 and 90 lb. Then quite suddenly the hook plinked out and Nanda's line fell slack. Obviously I find it impossible to paraphrase in writing what a certain woman said at that precise moment, though I admit my sentiments were the same – so near and yet so far . . .

At 4 pm we were back at the river again to fish from my favourite centre rock. No sooner had I put out chilwa on a long cast and allowed my attentions to be drawn skywards to a pair of king vultures riding high on the thermals overhead, when down went the rod tip and out went a good 40 yards of line before I slammed the 9000 into gear. Twenty minutes later we landed a long chunky golden of 53 lb.

Half an hour before dark Suban suggested we try upstream where Nanda lost the big fish in the morning. And would you believe it the very same thing happened – a monster grabbed the chilwa on the first cast, taking off downstream and across through two sets of rocks and three small pools. This was a very ponderous fish, keeping deep to the black bedrock and only giving us a sight of its immense depth when it turned belly up competely exhausted into Suban's arms, having provided Nanda with a truly memorable 40 minute fight. Straight into the weigh sling it went before darkness completely beat us – 71 lb exactly and Nanda's best ever from the river. Somehow it seemed to make up for the monster she had lost earlier. Rowing the coracle back up against the flow, Suban's paddle suddenly broke, which immediately sent us into fits of laughter. Luckily the baler, a galvanised camping plate, served as a makeshift paddle and we made the opposite bank, laughing all the way back to camp.

Friday 16 Our last session and our last day in this wonderful valley and yes, our last hangover, all came around too quickly. Slowly without speaking we made the long walk across the rocks covering the flood plain so lush and green compared to the parched brown of the high hills above, down to the very bottom of the rapids. We sat contemplating the majesty of it all while Suban and Bola threw their cast nets into the shallow pools for chilwa. Once again Wilson managed to botch a really thundering take on the first cast, but the second, with the line hung out behind a large rock so the bait was presented in the slack behind, I did not miss. Down to the end of the pool went the mahseer, promptly

Facing page: As Nanda finally attempted to battle a mahseer away from the white water into the waiting arms of Suban, the only way of capturing the action was to clamber over rocks below the fish with the waterproof Nikon.

Left: The mahseer, a golden of 41 lb, lies totally exhausted while Suban carefully removes the size 6/0 hook. It accepted an eight inch barbel dead bait bounced between the rocks in only four feet of turbulent white water.

Nanda has every right to look happy with her prize 71 lb golden mahseer, which requires Suban's help to hold up for the camera following a memorable fight. It some-how seemed to make up for the monster she lost earlier.

wrapping the line around a large group of sizeable boulders, and then all went tight. Suban as usual was quick to the rescue, swimming out to free the line which allowed me to enjoy a fight with what was to be our last mahseer of this year's trip, a golden of exactly 45 lb.

Back in camp we enjoyed our last lunch, had a long, long swim and took a last reflective look across the wide river in front of the camp to a part of the world that will forever be in my subconscious for a hundred and one reasons. Saying goodbye to Suban and Bola was, as usual, an emotional moment when I suppose I come as near to tears as I ever do. To fish in their company and be taught so many fundamental principles about the river and its entanglement of black bedrock, the fish and other wildlife makes me feel very humble indeed. Nanda accompanied us on the long, dusty drive back to the city where the big bird was due to take off at 17.50 hours. I would rather have been back at the river watching the vultures.

Warm and sunny. Light north-westerly, breeze.

Having spent the weeks after the Indian interlude knocking the back lawn, flower beds and the herbage around the two lakes into shape, not to mention organising stock for a new spring and summer season in the tackle shop, I suddenly felt the need to get away from it all and go trout fishing. There was a time when I never missed the start of a new trout season on April 1st, but in recent years having spent the run up out in India mahseer fishing, that urgency had been missing. Perhaps I am at last slowing down. Anyway, along with Charlie Clay and Nobby Clarke who were round at the house by 11.30 am we set off, first stop being the Buckinghamshire Arms at Blickling for a pub lunch and a couple of glasses.

Eventually at around 2 pm we arrived at Bure Valley trout fisheries in North Norfolk in brilliant sunshine with only a slight ripple blowing the length of the three interconnected lakes. The weather may have been wonderful, but I fancied the fishing would be gruelling. It was. On past form we decided to fish the largest lake which Dave Green the owner usually stocks with a larger stamp of both brown and rainbows, and after a quick natter with him at the lodge we made our way over to the north bank, adjacent to which flows the lovely River Bure. In these high upper reaches its pure water can be crossed in a jump. What a contrast to the hustle and bustle of the river lower down in its wide, coloured reaches at holiday centres like Wroxham, only 20 miles away. In fact this particular lake, or rather pit, was featured in one of the trout fishing programmes in the *Go Fishing* television series. It was actually being excavated at the time and a long way from being allowed to fill up from the water table and mature into a fishery. I took great pleasure when I saw that in just two years, the bankside had grown quite colourful with more than a splash of bright yellow from the vigorously self-seeding gorse and broom.

With an enormous hatch of land-born hawthorns coming off (those big jet-black, hairy flies with the characteristic dangling rear legs), we initially thought we were in for a real bean feast. Trout were rising freely on the edge of the ripple some 25 yards out where the hawthorns were being blown. However our imitations provoked only the occasional rise. So, after an hour or so Charlie and I played a crafty move. We walked round to the opposite bank and rowed the boat out to the narrow island which put us bang in the middle of the strongest ripple. Here we started to take fish immediately on black buzzers and small black sedges tweaked gently through the surface film. However, sport was rather short-lived. After taking a couple of rainbows apiece to around the 2 lb mark and dropping the same, the ripple all but went and the trout retreated well beyond our casting range. Poor old Nobby had to log up a total blank, which for such a seasoned fly fisherman is most unusual. Nevertheless even he agreed it was lovely to be out again and chew the fat with old friends.

Thursday 24

Very warm and sunny all day with hardly a trace of wind.

U pon writing today's entry and looking at the date of the previous one, I realise that over a month has elapsed since I last wet a line. Not that I haven't made the most of spring by the waterside – far from it – walking the dogs twice a day around my lakes and feeding the carp and ducks with bread scraps more than fulfills that strange craving anglers have for being near water. In fact, like most fishery owners at this time of year, I have been busy pruning back foliage along the pathways and generally tidying up the swims in readiness for the new coarse fishing season ahead. As a result, fly fishing trips have gone by the by.

However I did get out and enjoyed a spell of spotty fishing down in Hampshire at the beautiful Leominstead Fishery on the edge of the New Forest with Tania, my girlfriend. The last time we fished together was almost 24 years ago and it was probably my fascination for the sport in those days which rather abruptly ended our romance after nearly two years together. So now, second time around since we coincidentally met up again back in January, I have naturally been reticent in pushing fishing too far. . . yet!

We stayed overnight in Stockbridge, meeting up for dinner with Andy Davison and Julie who had also driven down from Norfolk, and my old mate Trevor Housby and his wife Islda plus 10-year-old son Russel. Now it could have been something to do with the way in which the wine was flowing both during and after dinner which dulled my enthusiasm for

Why is it that beginners always seem to do better with trout than the experts? Young Russel Housby tied the fly, Tania caught the trout and fellow angling author Trevor Housby netted it from the beautiful Leominstead Fishery on the edge of Hampshire's New Forest. Wilson blanked.

pulling a fly through the water, or it might have been that I merely wanted Tania to be catching the trout. Either way, after half an hour of explaining to Tania the best method of retrieving, I could not induce one pull on the yellow eyed damsel fly nymph that young Russel Housby had very kindly tied up for the occasion. Clear skies, strong sunlight and a flat calm obviously did little to improve matters, so I cast out again, handed the rod to Tania and turned away to natter with Trevor, which of course was exactly what someone up there wanted me to do. Not having gone two yards, out of the corner of one eye I saw the line tighten as Tania started the retrieve, followed moments later by a rainbow leaping high into the air. There followed a lively tussle with Tania grinning throughout like a cheshire cat and playing the trout pretty well, till Trevor did the honours with net and priest.

Fish were obviously in the area so Wilson claimed the rod back and tried another few casts, again without a pull or so much as a follow in. Then, quite dramatically, Trevor's rod which had been leaning against the lower limb of a Rhododendron bush for a good half hour doing nothing buckled in half, the reel screeching wildly. Trevor nonchalently walked up and handed the rod to Tania who now got the chance to play her second fish. Trevor's presentation consisted of a buoyant booby fly fished on a short cast so that it hung suspended two feet above the sunken line which lay along the bottom – pop-up ledgering you could say. The theory is that whenever a trout swims close to this static fly its tail movement imparts life to the artificial and the trout swallows it. Once Trev had removed the fly – completely out of sight down the trout's throat – put his rod down again after casting and lay back in the sun, I did the same. I gave the rod back to Tania who once again, believe it or not, got fast into yet another 2 lb plus rainbow, but unfortunately this one shed the hook just when she was getting the better of it. What a shame!

Wilson could stand the heckling from his mates no longer and had another go, figuring that Tania's lucky secret lay in the fact that quite a few seconds elapsed between my casting and handing the rod over to her, by which time of course the leaded nymph would be much closer to the bottom before she started the retrieve. Yes! Wilson was now on his way, and I yanked the line back for a brisk double haul cast to put the nymph way out there into the deep gully which ran parallel to the bank some 20 yards out. But it was not my day. As I punched through on the forward cast the rod snapped off with a resounding crack! just above the spigot and the top joint slithered down the flapping line straight into the lake. Well at least it brought the house down, and improved Andy and Julie's day because they had taken only one fish. Housby, having taunted me mercilessly all morning nearly split his belly laughing. Tania wasn't sure about how I would react, but soon joined in once she saw I too could only see the funny side. Laughing at one's own misfortune is an ability which you must have to be able to make the most of fishing.

27 Sunday

Warm and sunny. No wind.

This morning's escapade cannot truly be regarded as a fishing trip, even though I spent three hours in the water squeezed into a wet suit that I swear shrinks every year. It was the annual lily clear out at Rackheath Springs near Wroxham, something I am silly enough to do prior to the start of each new season simply because no one else fancies the job, even though I haven't actually tried for carp here for several seasons now. The thing is (but don't tell anyone) I actually enjoy the exercise, and the excess roots of the common yellow water lilies which would otherwise cover the shallow lake's surface from bank to bank (had I not been cutting them back for the last 10 years) are certainly not wasted. They have been distributed to dozens of new and existing gravel pit fisheries all over Norfolk, including my own lakes. Removing them is a simple job, providing you like being armpit deep in foul smelling silt, the result of accumulated leaf fall from the tall oaks, alders and poplars bordering the lake. A well sharpened bagging hook is used to slice through the leg sized rhizomes within 18 inches of the crown. This leaves a rooted plant complete with pads, flowers and the soft subsurface lettuce-like leaves, ready for replanting into a new home.

Friend Charlie Clay helped with the operation and brought his trailer along so that we could take a load of lilies back to

Donning a wet suit and wading about in the deep silt of a local club water to thin out tough roots of the yellow water lily is a close season pastime of the author. The excess roots are not wasted, they are transplanted to other local fisheries.

Lenwade for the Bridge Lakes Club syndicate run by fellow Norwich tackle dealer Tom Boulton, once members from other clubs had collected their quota. After two hours of hard work we had filled the boat. It was lovely to see so many carp moving about, some at incredibly close quarters, as they inspected the strange creatures disturbing their normally tranquil residence.

Our appetites for the coming season having been well and truly whetted, Charlie and I deposited a good fifty roots back in Lenwade, but no one was there to plant them. Tom is a crafty so and so. He probably thought that if he turned up late Wilson would be silly enough to plant them, which of course I did. The sun was so incredibly strong I feared they would dry up if we simply left them at the waterside, and I was not about to let all our hard work go to waste. Incidentally, here is a good method for anyone wishing to secure lilies into a lake bottom, whether it consists of mud, silt or gravel. Work a spade back and forth to form a wedge-shaped cavity and press the root in with your foot, rocking the spade back and forth again as it is lifted out. The root then becomes very firmly embedded and is usually impervious to the attentions of large species such as carp, which are always irresistably attracted to the introduction of new plants and try their utmost to uproot them.

13 Wednesday

Overcast all day.
Rather chilly wind.

Due to the amount of work involved in ensuring that all is ready for action in the tackle shop, the last few weeks leading up to the start of a new coarse fishing season always seem to fly by. The evenings have been busy too, spent cutting back dense marginal growth and clearing the pathways leading down to each swim around the two carp lakes in front of the house. Being a month ahead of herself this year, due to the mild winter and early spring, nature has provided an unseasonally vigorous growth of brambles, willows, gorse, broome and alders. The colourful wild flowers that anglers associate with June and July are actually all just about finished, particularly rhododendrons, the yellow iris and foxgloves. I hope the syndicate members who fish the lakes don't feel cheated by the lack of early season colour.

At least the fishing should prove consistent, the majority of carp spawned way back during the heatwave at the beginning of May, and have been piling the weight back on since then. However I will not spend the early hours of 16th June with the carp in my own lakes, I shall leave them to the syndicate members, in preference for the specimen bream which inhabit a local Wensum Valley gravel pit complex and have held my attention now for the start of several seasons. It was here, in this interesting complex of pits joined together by small streams and bisected by countless tree clad islands, that Charlie Clay and I spent this evening, looking for bream shoals. Due to varying densities of weed growth each new season which affect the fishability of at least half the potential bream-producing swims, our pre-season reconnaissance trips invariably prove worthwhile. After all, there is little merit in turning up on spec in the dark on opening morning, only to find weed from top to bottom in your chosen spot once the sun gets up. Armed with catapults, binoculars, polaroids, chest-high waders and a good supply of sweetcorn and stewed wheat for prebaiting, we spent a fascinating three hours trying to work out where we would begin our attack. Not that we ever expect to improve upon the red letter morning of last year's opening when bream weighing 10 lb 12 oz and 11 lb 5 oz fell to my rod on successive casts, with another of 8 lb 12 oz shortly afterwards, not to mention 5 lb 6 oz tench. That first bream came to ledgered breadflake, the others on float fished sweetcorn presented lift style over a bed of the same. I had waited so many years finally to put the net beneath a double figure bream, catching two in the same session almost confused the elation I felt.

The small shoals of very large bream inhabiting this particular complex of pits have grown to such proportions because there are no competition species other than tench. Moreover because the water in each pit is nearly always gin clear, they can invariably be tracked down visually. Not that the bream will necessarily feed, but at least reconnaissance gives us the opportunity of fishing where they actually live as opposed to waiting for a group to find a prebaited area on each and every trip. They also oblige by rolling on the surface at dawn and dusk. This was why Charlie and I sat the evening out almost into darkness hoping the chilly wind would die, the surface calm off and the bream start showing themselves. In the event this is exactly what happened.

In the middle of the shallow lake several good fish started porpoising. Two swims were within easy casting range from the bank and another from a tiny island requiring waist-high waders to reach. In fact it was the same swim which produced the goods for me last year, but we intend to wait till Saturday morning to decide which ones to choose. With an advance weather forecast for the weekend promising temperatures considerably higher than the past week, especially at night, along with warmer winds, the omens for a good start seem promising. Let's hope so.

Having carefully waded out through the clear waters of the pit to a position from where the patrol routes of the bream shoal can be covered, Charlie Clay starts to get among the whoppers on the glorious 16th June. The successful method is ledgered breadflake.

For many of the fishermen who patiently wait three months for the new coarse season to arrive, the so-called 'glorious 16th of June' does not always fulfil its promise. Therefore, after a particularly successful opening session this morning, Charlie Clay and I can feel justifiably happy, because our pre-fishing reconnaissance paid handsome dividends in some lovely bream, several missed chances and a real surprise catch. I must admit however, that getting up early is becoming harder; waking to the sound of the wretched alarm at 2.30 am after only two hours sleep was most unwelcome. Serves me right for hitting the sack late I suppose.

We had arranged to meet at the water but in the event we both arrived in the car park at the same time, and after

16 Saturday

Warm and sunny all day.
No wind.

Charlie Clay came close to the jackpot during the early hours by netting two bream in excess of nine pounds before hitting his long-awaited first double figure bream – a beautifully conditioned and unusual two-tone specimen, tipping the scales at exactly 10½ lb.

unloading the gear quietly from our cars we eagerly made our way through the thick mist. Our destination was the favourite middle lake where the bream had been rolling on Wednesday evening. On the way we almost trod on a hedgehog who peered into Charlie's torch beam, disgruntled at being disturbed mopping up worms from the dew-soaked grass.

With such a drop in temperature overnight I was glad we had not chosen to fish all night, and fancied that the half a dozen syndicate members back at my carp lakes who had, would find sport rather on the slow side, as indeed they did. In recent years I have actually fared better by rising early and relatively fresh after a few hours sleep to start as dawn breaks, than waking up shivering in the early hours by the waterside, all motivation gone. Nothing saps strength and interest more quickly than feeling freezing cold. By this regime I can fit in

It was a red-letter day for both Charlie and myself – I took bream to close on 9 lb, plus this huge 5 lb 1 oz roach/bream hybrid, the largest I have ever seen in nearly 40 years of freshwater fishing.

two, sometimes three pre-work early mornings per week, whereas one exhausting all-nighter would be all I could manage in that time.

Wading out to my favourite 'island' swim, a precarious task even in daylight because of the silt-filled pot holes in the gravel bottom, was simply not feasible, so I opted for a piece of sloping bank at the deeper eastern end of the four acre lake, thickly fringed in sweet reed grass and sedge. Charlie disappeared into the mist around the northern bank emerging at a shallow plateau where by careful wading he could place both baits over a wide area just beyond the range attainable from my chosen swim. This resulted in the entire middle section of the lake being covered in exactly the area where the bream had been rolling on Wednesday evening. As luck would have it, the beauties had not moved.

Within minutes of putting two rods out on buzzers and luminous bobbins, one rig at 30 yards and the other at around 50 yards with a breadflake and cage feeder holding coarse crumbs presented on each, the action started. Or rather that age-old problem associated with ledgering for deep-sided species such as bream in shallow weedy waters – the dreaded line bite syndrome – began. Time after time the bobbin jingled up and down as bream accidentally picked the line up with their large fins. As always it was a case of striking repeatedly at anything slow and positive and treating those missed – which most were – philosophically, as 'liners'.

For a good three hours, despite being just 100 yards away to the right, the density of the mist prevented me from actually seeing how Charlie was faring, though every now and then I heard the swish of a strike and the faint 'bleep bleep bleep' from his Optomics, followed by unprintable exclamations.

To try to overcome the line bite problem I put a float rod up, because a bream is much less likely to bump into a few feet of line stretched vertically from float to bait, than 30 to 50 yards of horizontal line draped over weedbeds from rod tip to the ledger rig. The problem was, when casting to where the bream were situated, I couldn't see the float tip, so dense was the mist. So it was back to the double ledgering rod set-up, and the subsequent frustration of line bites. Three however, were not liners, despite the registrations on the bobbin indicator appearing no different. Suddenly, there was that lovely resistance on the rod tip at the end of the strike. The first resulted in a big, bronze-sided bream taking the dial scales down almost to 9 lb. It was a male fish covered in spawning tubicles, which for its weight looked considerably larger. The second, also a male which put up a spirited fight on 6 lb test (the hook length being 4 lb), came within a few minutes and weighed exactly a pound less. These were followed half an hour later after several more missed bites or line bites by a complete surprise. A whopping great roach/bream hybrid weighing an incredible 5 lb 1 oz. It was by far the biggest hybrid I have ever seen let alone caught and, incidentally, ever heard reported from Norfolk waters. A really dark, strangely coloured fish looking to all intents and purposes a good 80% bream, but also possessing the typical physical qualities of the roach. Like all hybrids, it fought like stink, far harder than both of the bream beforehand. It is a great pity the British Record Fish Committee do not include hybrids amongst their lists, for there is enormous interest and scope in this area.

Meanwhile, Charlie was really getting stuck in. I could hear the cursing across the lake as he too became increasingly frustrated by liners, repeatedly striking into thin air. But then suddenly over went his rod into a full curve and stayed there as a big bream found the breadflake and the size 10 hook went home. It was as though simultaneously, despite the areas we fished being 100 yards apart, the bream in each had suddenly started to get their heads down. It may well have been something to do with the drastic increase in light values, because the mist had now completely gone and the sun was shining brightly. Charlie's first bream turned out to be a real beauty of 9 lb 14 oz, by far his largest ever. This was followed by another cracker of 9 lb 7 oz, and just as I arrived at his swim with the camera bag, he belted into a tench. Well, Charlie said it was a tench. 'Yes John, it's a small tench', is how the patter went. 'Oh I don't know though, it could be a big tench. No it's not a tench, it's a bream. Only a small one though by the way it's fighting. I'm not so sure now', says Charlie, slipping the net beneath a real slab-sided beauty, 'It looks heavy and it's one of those odd looking "two tone" jobs.' He was of course referring to the bream's distinct colouration, where a vertical line separates colours of entirely different tones, but on one side of the fish only. A phenomenon which occurs more with bream than any other species, though I have seen both tench and pike similarly marked. Why this happens remains a mystery.

From the low angle at which I was banging away action shots on the Bronica using a wide angle lens and having waded out into the lake, the true size of the fish was not apparent. It was not until Charlie waded ashore with his prize, unscrewed the landing net top and hoisted it onto the dial scales, that I realised his ambition had at last been fulfilled. '10 lb 8 oz exactly' Charlie said, wading towards me with the bronze-sided beauty, 'My first double at last, John', and we shook hands warmly. I don't know who was more pleased, him or me.

Sunday 17

*Warm and sunny. Only a
few clouds in the sky.*

Had even more trouble rising this morning, eventually arriving at the lake a little after 4 am to find Charlie already fishing. Another angler was in my swim, so I rigged up to the right of Charlie, but as things turned out we might just as well have enjoyed a lie-in. The lake seemed totally dead, and as different from yesterday morning as it was possible to be. None of the four anglers who had been fishing the lake all night had wet their nets, or even so much as seen a bream roll. But that's bream fishing for you – all or nothing.

Sunday 24

*Sunny and warm all day.
Slight wind.*

This has certainly been a busy weekend. Lots of fishing combined with painting the kitchen, not that *I* managed to wet a line though.

Brother Dave, his wife Linda and two children came to stay, as did Tania and her 15-year-old daughter Hannah, who both had a field day with the roach in the lake at the bottom of the garden on Saturday evening. In fact I had been prebaiting this particular deep swim with peanuts for nearly three weeks, introducing a pint of nuts morning and evening. I had already observed big tench and the odd carp mopping up baits from the edge of the shelf where the gravel bottom plummets dramatically from two feet in the margins, to over twelve feet only two rod lengths out. However the regular prebaiting had also attracted a huge shoal of roach into the swim, all going so potty over nuts that a one swan shot lift float rig never had a chance to reach bottom. A size 8 hook holding a jumbo American peanut might not seem the ideal size roach bait, but Tania and Hannah were pulling them out to well in excess of 1½ lb, taking it in turns with the float rod. The following morning, Dave rose early to fish the same spot and took over 30 fish of similar proportions and lost something huge which promptly straightened the forged size 8. Most probably a carp.

When, after a late breakfast the decorating finally started, Dave's absence was soon conspicuous as was the half-finished ceiling. Of course we all knew immediately that he had slunk off to one of the carp lakes, and sure enough after a while he

emerged panting at the back door asking for me to come and photograph a mirror carp he had just caught which weighed 15 lb 6 oz. Then, and only then, did we all finally get stuck into the kitchen. In fact it was good of them to come up to Norfolk and help me with the decorating in readiness for a party Tania and I had planned for next weekend. No doubt Dave will be fishing again then. As things turned out we never did completely finish the painting, so I expect my fishing next week will suffer as a result.

Above left: One minute Dave was painting the kitchen ceiling, the very next he was landing a 15 lb carp.

Above right: Fishing a swim which John had been pre-baiting with peanuts, Tania soon started pulling out plump roach to well over the pound on a single jumbo American peanut fished lift style.

Thanks to yesterday's marathon of painting and fishing, I had great difficulty rising at 3 am this morning. In fact I couldn't, and it was well past four o'clock when, complete with carp tackle, I finally found myself on the way to a lovely little estate lake south of Norwich, partially revived by a mug of black coffee drunk en route. By the time I arrived at the long, shallow, reedy lake which I call the 'Warblers' (due to the thick reedy margins harbouring a respectable

25 Monday

Humid, hazy and overcast. Slight westerly breeze.

colony of these interesting little birds) the early morning 'bubbling' from the carp had long since finished. Serves me right. Nevertheless, there were a few lone fish still to be seen moving about and thus susceptible to the stalking, roving approach that suits the overgrown features of this particularly clear lake. The depth can be measured in mere inches at the western end where the feeder stream enters, completely hidden in a thicket of alders, willows and common reed. Patches of reed and iris then alternate along both banks mixed with sedge and rush, towards the dam end by the outlet, where the deepest water is just four feet. Location is therefore not much of a problem, but approaching and then extricating big fish from a heavy growth of soft weeds and lilies provides a continual challenge, which is why I love the lake so. A proportion of the carp stock, which includes several huge mirrors to over 30 lb were actually visible, but these remained indifferent to small quantities of loose feed; neither were they interested in my float fished particle baits, peanuts or tiger nuts.

Previous years at the Warblers have seen me taking carp to 27¼ lb, plus several other 20 lb plus fish. But a 30 lb specimen (and I know they exist because at least two different fish have been taken), has yet to grace my net although two summers ago I did part company with a particularly huge mirror in the reeds after a long and arduous battle. By 8.30 am when it was time to head back to Norwich and the shop, at least two large carp had inspected the baits closely (within inches) without the slightest trace of interest. It was as though the hook bait did not exist.

As the day was so humid I fancied there might still be a chance of the carp feeding at some time and so I revisited the lake for three hours after work until 8 pm. However my hay fever made concentration impossible, and after marring my approach towards fish feeding earnestly in the margins by crunching too heavily through the sedges, I reluctantly headed for home, puffy-eyed and absolutely exhausted. What a frustrating day's fishing!

There was not much fishing done last week as a result of kitchen painting in readiness for last night's party. Having cleaned up the aftermath of entertaining 150 guests, Tania and I finally hit the sack around 4 am whilst brother Dave was fumbling around in the garage threading 6 lb line through the rings on his 11 foot Avon in preparation for a dawn attack on the carp. And he was not alone: several house guests had in fact planned to fish immediately the bash had quietened down. Frankly they were welcome, with the wind howling through the tall oaks adjacent to the house, accompanied by the rain literally sheeting down. I took a long look before shutting the garage door after Dave so the dogs couldn't wander off and nick anyone's bait, and reflected that 10 years ago I would have been just as keen and joined him despite a hangover. Nowadays, well, I guess I know when I have had enough.

Martin Founds and his wife Jean, of *Anglers World Holidays*, had travelled down from Derbyshire especially for the party and so that we could go over the final travelling arrangements prior to the start of filming another *Go Fishing* series (*Go Fishing* 5 and 6 no less), the first of which we shoot in Canada in just two weeks time. We checked and re-checked our itinerary, considering the time we would have between flights in the two locations high up in the provinces of the North West Territories and Manitoba. With only ten actual days of filming in a fifteen day round trip, capturing the action of catching arctic grayling, giant lake trout, northern pike and channel catfish, plus wildlife fill-ins will, I think, prove rather tight. But it's a challenge I relish and am really looking forward to now that we are finally on our way. Of course everything has been a last minute rush, with nothing absolutely certain till only a week ago when Anglia Television finally gave their written confirmation to our production unit, which consists of Gelly Morgan, Paul Martingel and myself. Unlike the previous four series of *Go Fishing* which were organised by an independent producer/director, we now have very definite ideas as to how we can extend fishing on television into a more visually exciting and informative format, yet retain the relaxed form of presentation for which *Go Fishing* has become so well known. That's the theory anyway, we shall have to see how it works out.

1 Sunday

Rain, sunny intervals.
Gusty westerly wind.

Tuesday 3

Still, cold dawn followed by strong sunlight. Light westerly wind.

Following a hectic tussle through weed beds and tree roots, John finally has a Warblers lake carp safely in the net. This one was hooked on float fished peanuts, presented lift style just five yards out.

Much of my carp fishing is enjoyed during the early hours before opening the tackle shop in Norwich. I may lose sleep, but catching beautifully coloured carp like this 21¾ lb golden mirror makes it all worthwhile.

With the temperature having fallen rapidly yesterday evening, I instinctively fancied an early session at Warblers lake. The chill and heavy mist would, I suspected, find at least a few carp bubbling away for an hour or two from dawn onwards, as indeed they were. After setting the alarm for 2.45 am I was comfortably settled in a little before four o'clock beneath a tall weeping chestnut at the deeper end of the lake, to where all floating natural food is blown when the wind comes from the west. By kneeling low to the ground and holding the binoculars steady, even in the half light of dawn it was not difficult to make out the gentle 'bulging' on the surface as great backs foraged through the beds of millfoil and hornwort in just three feet of water. Upon the thickly curdled surface – a mixture of leaves, pollen and dead moths, plus the flattened feeding bubbles of tench and carp from several hours past – small clusters of new bubbles could be seen spewing to the surface not 20 feet out from the dam.

I scattered in a couple of dozen jumbo American peanuts (a large particle bait I particularly favour because their buoyancy means that they lie on top of the weed or soft silt instead of falling through and being hidden) and relaxed for a few minutes keeping a close eye on the bubbles to interpret in which direction each carp was moving. Matched to the 12 foot 1¾ lb test curve carbons was an 11 lb line fixed with a peacock quill lift rig, a single swan shot pinched on five inches from the size 4 hook holding a single nut. The tackle was flipped out less than two rod lengths with an underarm swing and when the quill settled half cocked indicating the shot was indeed on the bottom, I wound down till just an inch of the float protruded above the surface. With the float positioned halfway between two sets of bubbles (casting right on top of a feeding carp is the quickest way of frightening it) I was almost expecting instant action, so I held the rod for quick strike and haul tactics. But the carp were not having any, and made me wait with nerve ends at fever pitch for fully an hour and a half before one of them sucked in the peanut.

One second the float was there, the next it was not. So fast had the carp moved off, the rod was almost wrenched from my grasp before the old brain gave the message to strike. Fortunately with such aggressive bites the carp actually hooks itself, and within seconds this particular fish had travelled 25

yards to my left where the sunken branches of a fallen willow spelt certain danger. Immediately I thrust two thirds of the rod beneath the surface to lower the angle of line between fish and rod tip, this seemed to do the trick and the carp harmlessly skirted the partly submerged branches without that nasty grating feeling coming up the line. This was obviously a big fish, for I could do nothing except hang on and give line reluctantly as it ploughed through a weed bed going down the centre channel. It went chugging off up the lake but was by now almost exhausted and I started to gain line. Finally it came quietly to the surface ready for netting, a lovely thick-set, golden mirror looking all of 20 lb plus. In fact, it took the spring balance down to 21 lb 12 oz exactly.

After sacking the carp to photograph later, I left the dam end to quieten down and slowly meandered along the lake up towards the shallow end, but saw only the small area of bubbling carp adjacent to an enormous patch of white lilies. These I covered with the lift rig and peanuts and within a few minutes the float moved positively and slowly under. I rather think it must have been a 'liner' (a carp picking up the line around its dorsal or large pectoral fins) because as I whacked the rod up in a long, hard, sweeping strike, the surface suddenly erupted as though a cow had fallen in. At least two huge fish; it could even have been three or four, went charging off down the lake leaving enormous furrows in their wake as the float rig catapulted back over my head into the trees minus the bait. And that was it, I could see nothing else moving anywhere in the lake after a good half an hour with the binoculars, and so happily drove into Norwich and the shop (late again) after taking a few trophy shots of the big mirror and returning it. Things are looking up.

Thursday 5

Overcast and raining. Bitterly cold north-westerly wind.

Why on earth I revisited Warblers lake this morning heaven only knows. I should have taken heed and seriously considered the weather for once, because having risen again at 3 am less than an hour later I was fishing, wishing I'd stayed in bed. For an hour I stuck the cold facing wind at the dam end where I took the big mirror two mornings back, but without the slightest sign of bubbles or fish. Eventually I could stand shivering no longer, and by 5.30 am I was glad to be back in bed again.

T hough I personally did not catch a thing and had no intention of doing so, today's fishing proved to be far more rewarding than anything I could ever have wished to catch. The 'Dreams Come True' charity asked me to provide a day's fishing to 13 year old David Wright who, after receiving two years of chemotherapy for bone cancer, was at last on the mend. Of course, with two carp lakes literally within a stone's throw of the house, I was delighted to oblige. In fact it was an ideal opportunity to double up on another request from the *Star* newspaper to fish with 12 year old James Hore from Leavenheath in Suffolk, who had won a sponsored prize and chosen yours truly.

David and Tony his father drove down from Stockport near Manchester, staying overnight at the Lenwade House Hotel who very kindly provided complimentary accommodation and meals for the occasion. At 10 am sharp they were round at the house as arranged.

The idea was to put a few carp David's way before James and his dad, Peter, who had a comparatively short drive from Suffolk, arrived at lunchtime. But the best laid plans often go wrong. On any other occasion I would have bet my back teeth (those I have left) that David would have landed a double figure carp within an hour. The lakes are that well stocked. Lady luck however was all against this plucky young fisherman, who hooked no less than four carp all well into double figures on both floating and bottom baits, because for various reasons each one came adrift.

As a consolation prize he did manage to keep the hook in a mirror carp of about 4 lb which accepted float fished luncheon meat just before lunch – a barbecue on the back lawn prepared by Tania and Hannah. Thank heavens the weather held.

It was my intention that in addition to enjoying a day out in the countryside in our lakeland setting, the two boys

8 Sunday

Sunny all day. Gusting westerly wind.

actually learnt something about stalking and the opportunist way of catching carp. So I had them stealthily crawling about casting to patches of bubbles, offering floating baits to surface patrollers, freelining pastes into the lilies and so on. I think, to be fair, it was all a bit beyond them, but they put up with my insistence and banter exceptionally well. Shortly after lunch, young James after placing his crust between two patches of lilies and botching two chances, finally connected with a fine common carp which led him a real song and dance for over ten minutes. In the background behind the camera, Wilson could be heard issuing orders and directions ten to the dozen (could not bear the thought of him losing the fish) and eventually David did the honours for James by putting the net expertly beneath 12 lb of glistening, immaculate carp and

Despite having lost several good fish himself, David Wright from Stockport (right) willingly nets a 12 lb common for James Hore of Leavenham during a day's fishing on the author's carp lakes organised by the charity Dreams Come True.

heaving it up onto a bed of sedges. I doubt the fish had ever been caught before, so perfect were its fins and pattern of scales, and of course, young James just couldn't believe his good fortune.

After all the commotion we moved down to the house end of the new lake for a final assault late in the afternoon. But it was just not going to be David's day. He suffered two more lost fish, one a very large mirror which slurped up nonchalantly to take his floater and promptly shot off at top speed when the hook went home. To stop the carp finding refuge in a thick bed of sedges fringing the opposite bank, David was forced into applying excessive pressure, and the line snapped. Words are little use to a young, terribly disappointed fisherman experiencing so many set backs on his big day out, but we had given it more than our best shot and I hope he will remember the fun we had along the way. To see the look on a youngster's face when he first hooks into a whopper and feels that unstoppable power which quickly makes his arm ache, is infinitely more rewarding than catching fish yourself. Believe me.

Several days ago the thought suddenly dawned on me that so far this season I had not enjoyed a single outing after tench, and as I required extensive photographic material on the species for a forthcoming book, the decision was to kill two birds with one stone and ring Charlie Clay to see if he fancied a trip out. Our choice was a beautiful estate lake of some 20 acres set in deepest North Norfolk and surrounded at the dam end by tall oaks, beech and ash trees; a lake I first fished with Charlie some 15 years ago when he still had hair on the top of his head and when mine was still brown. Our day out is actually chronicled in a diary book I wrote that year (1976) called *A Specimen Fishing Year*, now, of course, long out of print. Because of the lake's breathtaking setting I also chose this particular location for the very first programme of the *Go Fishing* series, and have not revisited its tench population since then – exactly five years ago to the week. So having picked Charlie up at 3.30 am sharp for a dawn start and so that we could enjoy an early drive through the estate

12 Wednesday

Baking hot and sunny all day. Variable south-westerly wind.

Below: To keep the tench rooting about, Charlie Clay lays down a carpet of sweetcorn by catapult.

Below right: Early season tench and the lift method go together like peaches and cream. Light float fishing is always more effective than ledgering because of the greater degree of sensitivity.

and around the lake while the deer were still about, we were indeed curious as to whether the tench were as prolific as they used to be, when up to 20 fish of between 3 and 5 lb at a sitting was not an uncommon haul.

Many anglers, and indeed the public in general, tend to moan about the existence of large, privately owned estates, which is a great pity because were it not for these wildlife havens, our countryside would eventually become abused beyond repair. These are perhaps sad facts, but borne out by all those coarse fisheries which are available to the general public either free, or on a day-ticket basis. Collectively, people do unfortunately tend to leave litter and trample down bankside flowers, abusing that which is beautiful to others. Nor are they always quiet, caring and tolerant of wildlife. Of course for every one careless visitor there are many, many anglers who respect the environments in which they enjoy their sport.

Anyway, back to our drive. We bumped through narrow tracks bordering several pine plantations, across which a

thousand rabbits hopped, plus one single dog fox. Finally we came out onto the huge sloping meadow beside the lake where hundreds of deer scampered out of the way and then stopped stock still to stare with curiosity while I gently eased the Saab along a deeply rutted track down to the water's edge, hoping it wouldn't cost me yet another new exhaust system.

Mist was still rising as Charlie unloaded the gear while I took the binoculars for a walk around the dam end looking for the bubbles of feeding tench. The effects of the unusually dry summer immediately ruled out at least half the lake; much of the shallow end where a stream normally enters was bone

Having had the entire lake all to ourselves, we ended the session at lunch time with seven good tench in the net – the largest to Charlie's rod at 5¾ lb.

93

dry, with mussel shells plainly high and dry where there was once two feet of water and in previous summers, large groups of feeding tench. So we settled in at the dam end, choosing a shallow area out in the middle for the feeder rods, and a deep gully next to the dam itself for a spot of lift method float fishing. Now you would naturally assume that with only 100 yards between these two spots the tench would be of a similar mood in each. But not on your nelly!

I sat for two frustrating hours in vain trying to tempt a positive bite from tench, bubbling heartily away in ten feet of water almost beneath the rod tip, on handfuls of loose fed maggots and sweetcorn. An initial helping of the same was added to breadcrumb ground bait at dawn. At first Charlie was faring similarly on the feeder rods, with just the very occasional twitch. I assumed that with the water being so very clear (you could actually see mussel shells on the bottom six feet down at 5 am) we were really on a hiding to nothing. But then, as the sun hit the weedy shallows to where Charlie was directing his feeders, the tench suddenly started feeding in earnest, taking the ledger bobbins up to the butt ring in really positive style, whereas, from just three semi-hittable dips of a light lift float rig down at the dam outlet, I could only keep the hook in one solitary tench (after losing the first). Fortunately it was a nice female of almost 5¼ lb which put up a superb scrap on the 14 foot match rod and 3 lb line.

By now I could stand Charlie's comments of 'getting loads of bites now, John' or 'just pulled out of another one', no longer, and reluctantly put the float rod away. I had planned to keep the cameras buzzing and that was impossible situated so far away from Charlie, so I whacked out two feeder rigs and enjoyed the fun from tench, which were onto the caster and maggot hook baits within a minute of the feeders settling amongst the carpet of soft bottom weed. While the 'hot' feeding area was between 60 and 70 yards out, situated roughly half-way was a particularly thick weed bed (a mixture of hornwort and blanket weed) which grew up through four feet of water almost to the surface, and in this we lost more tench than we extracted. This was I think, due to the feeder becoming firmly stuck, allowing the tench either to rip itself off the size 12 hook or actually break the 4 lb hook link. Rather frustrating, to say the least.

Nevertheless, we ended the session at lunchtime with seven good tench in the net, the largest coming to Charlie's rod at 5 lb 12 oz. This particular fish, a beautifully proportioned female, had a double set of nasty scars across its head and shoulder. Obviously there are some very large pike in the lake in addition to hordes of jacks up to 3 lb, one of which plagued Charlie and I all morning by grabbing our green, open-ended swim feeders on the retrieve, usually a few yards out from the bank. We knew exactly when it was about to attack from the instant 'jaws' type furrow which suddenly appeared in the wake of the feeder, and so boys being boys we played a few games with it. Twice it actually bit Charlie's feeder completely off and on one occasion came in so fast it ended up high and dry on the bank for a few seconds till it flipped back in again. Had we taken along a lure outfit and fished floating plugs, sport with pike would have been astounding, because all morning their long eruptions could be seen in the margins all around the lake.

CANADIAN ADVENTURE

15 **Sunday**

Since the coarse fishing season began it had been my intention to put in far more sessions prior to our filming in Canada than I have actually managed. Instead it will all have to wait till we get back to Britain. If anyone ever remembers, I should like to have etched on my gravestone the words 'He never had enough time'!

As I write, the Boeing 767 is flying smoothly over mid-Atlantic at 580 miles an hour and at a height of 33,000 feet, having completed half of the seven and a half hour flight from Gatwick to Toronto. Our film crew with myself, numbers six, including two members I haven't worked with previously, Melissa the production assistant and Henry the second cameraman (who, coincidentally, happens to be a Canadian living in Britain). Dave Lindsay, sound, and Paul Martingell, first cameraman/director both worked with me on series three and four of *Go Fishing*, while good friend Martin Founds, who has been responsible for organising the research side of these

The vastness of Canada's North West Territories, much of which is beneath ice for nearly nine months of the year, is difficult to comprehend. This area contains nearly ten per cent of the world's freshwater and the only means of transport available to the fisherman in these barren lands is the float plane.

programmes, comes along as co-ordinator and photographer.

Suddenly the enormity of the task ahead – making two half hour programmes from just nine days of actual fishing time, including long boat journeys and internal flights by float plane from one water course to another – has really dawned on me. It's a wonderful challenge though and we are lucky to have such exciting locations in Northern Canada for the first two programmes: the North West Territories which actually contain 9% of the world's freshwater, and Manitoba, known for its 100,000 freshwater lakes, most of which are uncharted and unnamed, but which contain unlimited stocks of arctic grayling and the world's biggest lake trout.

Following an overnight stay in Toronto at the Holiday Inn, at 10 am local time we boarded a 737 for a three hour flight, taking us directly across the Great Lakes in a north-westerly direction, to Winnipeg, where we checked our 26 piece filming luggage plus all our personal luggage into yet another Holiday Inn. I'm sure Martin must have shares in the company. In the afternoon we actually started work, although seasoned travellers would insist that travelling itself is actually more tiring, something about which I would certainly not argue. Our first location was Hawkins Taxidermy Studio in Winnipeg, where beautiful permatrophy replicas of fish which have been returned are hand-painted to perfection. In Canada most of the fishing lodges insist on barbless hook rules for a successful catch and release programme, so you simply measure the length and the girth of your specimen before returning it. Hawkins then do the rest and mail your trophy on when it's finished, to anywhere in the world. This is such a sensible attitude for a country which would seem to own a glut of fish-filled waters. They are obviously aware of how easily the balance could be upset by unthinking, uncaring fishermen, and have wisely decided to preserve this unique heritage for all time.

Our two hour flight out in the morning from Winnipeg to Rankin Inlet in the North Territories left at noon, and within half an hour of leaving Winnipeg and heading north, the scenery below started to change dramatically, the patchwork of suburbs and farmlands being replaced by a landscape of evergreens and water, and as the plane travelled further north, the number of lakes below grew steadily. We arrived in Rankin at 2.30 pm, the weather now noticeably much cooler, for the final leg of our long journey which should have been just an hour's flight by float plane to Ferguson Lodge.

Due to bad weather at Ferguson the plane was fogged in and we had to stay overnight. Keith Sharp, who runs Ferguson Lodge and who I had not seen since the World Travel Market back in London almost a year ago, lives in Rankin for most of the year. We were made very comfortable by Troy, a young Canadian who looks after Keith's home and business affairs during the exceptionally short summer fishing season from 'ice out' which does not happen this far north till the beginning of July, (we could see the odd iceberg in Hudson Bay as we landed in Rankin Inlet) to 'ice in' which occurs around the end of September. This leaves just an eight or nine week summer period for everything to happen, for Keith to make his profit, for the arctic wild flowers to propagate and bloom, and for the insects to reproduce, which is why mosquitoes and the dreaded black flies exist in such numbers.

The weather finally broke on Thursday morning, allowing us to make the one and a quarter hour flight to Ferguson Lodge. Because our transport was a 185 Cessna float plane, three trips were necessary, Paul, Dave and I taking the first leg, with Martin, Melissa and Henry (who then filmed our plane departing) going second. Due to the excessive luggage, Keith's pilot, Harvey, had to make a final trip in what can only be called 'passable' flying conditions.

During a fantastic caribou steak supper in the company of the six other fishermen staying at the lodge, Keith mentioned that in order for us to have two filming boats for tomorrow, he would need to move one from an outpost camp, where it had been left since last summer turned upside down with supplies beneath. This would necessitate a short trip in the Cessna followed by an overnight stop at Keith's new camp situated close to where we would be filming on the Kazan River. There was also mention of the fact that we would perhaps need to pull the aluminium boat over some ice floes, but Martin and I were so keen to start fishing that we volunteered gladly. Two hours later when Harvey dropped us where Keith had left the boat, complete with outboard engine fuel and fishing gear alongside the tiny island, we were shortly to experience the most terrifying time of our lives.

For the first thirty minutes the water was clear and I even had time to beach a few sizeable lakers. However as we set off towards the band of ice separating us from the outpost camp where we were to spend the night we realised the enormity of the task ahead. There was more than a mile of pack ice between our boat and clear water on the other side, and with the plane by now back at Ferguson, we had no option but to drag the boat over the ice floes or perish from exposure. Keith ran the bows of the boat right up onto the ice, which, he guaranteed, was perfectly safe to walk on and a good foot or so thick. So we all got out and pulled. Despite the hull weighing over 600 lb plus planks of timber, pots and pans and even a portable loo which had been left with other sundry supplies beneath the boat all winter, the aluminium boat slid quite freely over the ice. It even looked for a while as though we would soon be in the warm at Keith's outpost camp. Little did we know.

After an hour of pulling and pushing, dark areas of thin ice became far more numerous and we had to make long detours walking only on the firm, bright, white parts. Midnight quickly came and went, though of course, we could see easily because it never really gets dark this high up during the summer months. It did not, however, feel much like summer. Our hands were becoming painfully cold and we were starting to feel exhausted. We could see the clear water beyond the ice still a tantalising way off, yet we had no alternative but to plod on into the unknown.

Whenever the ice could be felt cracking beneath our feet, we immediately transferred most of our weight onto the boat by leaning across the gunnel. On the first occasion it actually gave way, Martin got his feet soaked (just a pair of trainers on, the silly sod) and then suddenly Keith, who was pulling and giving orders from up front, simply disappeared from view, all 23 stones of him, in a swirl that would not have disgraced a floundering hippo. Luckily, he managed to grab the side of the boat as the ice gave way and pull himself round the side till his feet were onto solid ice again. It was a very close shave indeed. Without Keith, Martin and I were goners and without us so was he. Not knowing if the next footstep would take us under the ice or keep us upon it, we became

With a beautiful sunset illuminating the horizon, pulling the boat across a wide ice floe seemed simple enough for Martin Founds, Keith Sharp and myself. Indeed the aluminium fishing boat was badly needed for the next day's filming. But danger awaited.

more and more anxious about our plight, especially when we saw the number of gaps now appearing between the ice floes, but Keith even had an answer for this predicament. The boat was pushed across the water from one chunk of ice to another to act as a portable bridge, and then pulled over after we had crossed. This technique is not as easy in practical terms as it is to describe. Whenever there was a mixture of mush and clear water we pushed the boat in, used the paddles and the engine for a few yards till we found solid walkable ice, and then ran the boat up again and continued onwards.

Throughout we were treated to a truly beautiful sunset as the great shining globe slowly sunk beneath the horizon, fusing the icy background into a multitude of colours;

variations of yellow, red and orange. The most curious thing of all was that even at two o'clock in the morning, as cold as it was out there on the ice, the mosquitoes were as thick as ever. It just did not make sense within my scheme of things, having to worry about being bitten whilst pushing a boat across ice floes. We were almost frozen to the bone when eventually, after five hours wondering if we were ever going to make it, we broke through the last ice floe into clear water. What a relief it was, and we hooted and whistled like three kids at a fun fair. There was then just a half hour's journey to Keith's outpost camp at Yathkyed where we had to wake up Rob, a young American who works for Keith all summer, to sort us out some bedding. After a brew of strong tea and a warm-up over the spirit stove, we finally got our heads down shortly before 4 am, completely and utterly knackered, and not a little lucky to be there at all.

Friday 20

Sunny and fairly windy all day.

Six days after leaving Gatwick, today was our first serious fishing and filming session. As arranged Harvey flew the rest of the crew in from Ferguson, and with all the gear stashed in the two boats we motored due west to Keith's favourite hot spot at the Kazan River junction. I soon understood why Keith wanted us to experience the challenge of this particular location. Two currents converge here forming a spectacular 200-yard wide pool with a boulder-strewn bed which varies in depth from six to more than twenty feet over a quarter of a mile.

After just three casts on camera, spinning on 15 lb test with a heavy spoon in the swirling and unbelievably clear water, over went the rod tip as a 20 lb lake trout grabbed hold. So aggressive was this particular fish that it actually slipped the barbless hook twice, grabbing hold again instantly and finally staying on for a fabulous head-shaking battle which included several arm-wrenching long runs against the clutch. To cut a long story short and because I caught so many beautiful big trout it is impossible to remember them all, sport was consistently excellent throughout the day, which, fortunately, remained bright and sunny – absolutely ideal for our filming requirements. Every so often I gave the fly rod an airing,

Whether using fly or spinning tackle, hitting into lake trout of 20 lb upwards is what brings fishermen to the clear, cold waters of Canada's North West Territories.

The laker is the largest trout in the world and it has been taken commercially to far in excess of the current rod and line record of 65 lb. However I was more than pleased with this 25 pounder taken on a wobbled spoon from the turbulent waters of the Kazan River junction.

Such was the head of huge trout collected in the Kazan River that even the TV film crew managed to get in on the action between takes. Martin Founds bends to net a 20 lb laker caught by sound recordist Dave Lindsay spinning from the shoreline.

using a fast sinking line and a large gaudy yellow and orange streamer which the jumbo lake trout simply adored. Some hit hard as the fly came around in the current in the traditional manner; some grabbed hold with unbelievable ferocity as the fly came around fast across the current, while others simply sucked the fly in greedily as it was being trailed just a few feet behind the boat.

At least a dozen lakers from 6 to 18 lb provided wonderful action for the cameras, and the fight from each on the fly outfit was really enjoyable. I could quite happily return to the Kazan River with nothing but a fly rod and a few dozen large

All good things must come to an end. The film crew reluctantly load up the Norseman float plane in preparation to leave Ferguson Lodge for the flight south into the province of Manitoba and Nueltin Lake.

flies; it is probably the most exciting location for fly fishing for huge trout anywhere in the world. The largest laker of all – a 25 pounder – fell to a heavy fluorescent yellow spoon worked slowly in fifteen feet of water in the late afternoon, an hour before we finished filming. It brought the tally of big lake trout weighing between 15 and 25 lb to a good dozen or more, though I honestly lost count of them all. Afterwards I calculated that I had actually spent less than four hours fishing both on and off camera. What an incredible day!

Unfortunately the weather changed yet again, which was a pity because throughout the morning Paul and I were putting the underwater camera through its paces and could have done with maximum light values. Nevertheless, the results of filming fish fighting and the action of lures and flies beneath the surface were encouraging. The lightweight camera is fixed to a pole and simply held down in the water as one would use a landing net. The camera is connected by cable to a video monitor through which I watched the results as a hooked fish was steered towards the boat.

After a shore lunch fry-up of lake trout, fresh bread and coffee, we motored down the Kazan River to a very promising set of rapids, with the intention of filming me catching grayling on the fly rod using a tiny spinner. As things turned

21 Saturday

Overcast, windy, rain all afternoon.

out I just couldn't stop hooking into big lake trout all upwards of 10 lb. It was all wonderful footage of course, but the only grayling was unfortunately taken off camera, and it was a real beauty too, a big male of fully 2¾ lb, its huge sail-like dorsal fin exquisitely dotted in aquamarine blue. The last trout I hooked 200 yards above the main rapids, and ended up losing it 200 yards below after an incredible fight on the fly rod and a tiny grayling spinner. It was at least a 30 pounder and I was as sick as a parrot because Henry had run the whole way with me, the heavy camera on his back, to capture the action. But so it goes. At 4 pm with the rain now bucketing down, we were not disappointed to hear the sound of Harvey's float plane but then had to take it in turns for the relay back to the lodge. Having drawn the second run, I was completely soaked to the skin by the time the Cessna returned.

Sunday 22

Sunshine followed by worsening rain.

We spent the morning shooting an ending to the programme with Keith chatting to me, and in the afternoon we shot a few grayling fill-ins.

After dinner Dave, Martin and I took a boat out over to a small inlet behind the camp to have a last try for the lake trout, and took seven between us on spoons. It was great fun and a nice end to our stay at Ferguson Lodge. In the morning we fly out to Nueltin Lake in the Norseman float plane which arrived late this afternoon. I had a word with Hap the pilot who I met last year at Nueltin and he mentioned the fishing there for pike and lake trout has been good. We shall see.

Monday 23

After torrential rain throughout the night, we breakfasted at seven thirty sharp and were loading up the Norseman float plane an hour later. I felt sad saying goodbye to Keith and his family after such a wonderful week – I could easily have stayed longer. We were not on holiday, however, and had to move on. With fine flying weather ahead we made the two and a quarter hour flight due south from Ferguson Lodge in the North West Territories to Nueltin in the Province of Manitoba, slightly ahead of time due to a strong tail wind. On arrival we were met by the owner Gary Gurke and Nap, the Chipaweyan Indian guide with whom Martin and I fished for a whole week last year when researching the area for television.

24 Tuesday

Warm and sunny all day.

Following a big, big Canadian-style breakfast, we all met down at the boat dock to shoot the introduction to the pike fishing part of the programme. The day was nothing less than glorious: blue skies, bright sunshine and colourful boats for the setting of shots. This took a good half hour, and we then motored up the lake for around 45 minutes to Nap's favourite pike location in the mouth of the Putahow River. The water was crystal clear and thick with weed beds in depths ranging from between four and eight feet. There were obviously lots of pike in all the bays we tried, but they were not exactly ravenous. Half-hearted stabs at our weedless lures were par for the course throughout the entire day, and though we boated around 10 small ones between 3 and 6 lb (Nap lost one double), I felt a trifle disappointed. However, the beautiful scenery and sunlight made up for the lack of big fish. You can't always have everything. Indeed, I think I get a little carried away thinking that I should be catching monster fish for the camera, when for much of the filming, they are probably not necessary; especially when the programme includes so many other interesting parts and breathtaking scenery. At noon, for instance, we filmed the traditional Canadian shore lunch of frying up our catch with chipped potatoes, onions and beans. It was delicious. Nap has a fabulous way of cleaning fish, leaving not the slightest trace of a bone in the fillets. He simply takes a big fillet off each flank, missing the main bone structure, then takes off the skin, leaving a fillet ready to be cut and rolled in a bag containing seasoned flour and dropped straight into a pan full of sizzling lard till golden brown. This works equally well with grayling and trout as it does with pike.

Wednesday 25

Sunny all day. Slight wind.

North American lake trout are unbelievably aggressive and will continue to hit the trolled spoon even if the barbless hook loses its purchase a couple of times. Trolled dead baits, big flies and diving plugs will also take them.

Although we have another two full days left after today here at Nueltin Lake, we really need them to shoot numerous fill-ins. Fortunately, we made an early start soon after breakfast and our three boats (two camera boats and the one I fished in) zoomed at over 25 miles an hour to one of Nap's favourite deep bays where the bottom shelves down to over 80 feet.

We first filmed the technicalities of down rigger trolling. This allows the lure to be trolled behind the boat at any depth by nipping the line 30 feet above the lure into the release clip of the down rigger ball (10 lb of lead connected to wire line from a special reel clamped to the gunnel) and lowering it down. On the Humminbird fish finder, several shoals of lakers were showing in the thermoclyne; that band of cold water between the bottom and the surface where a temperature of between 45° to 50° remains fairly constant all summer. We trolled round the bay until hits came, usually within 20 seconds of fish showing up on the screen. However it seemed that the trout were in an uncooperative mood, merely bumping into the big spoons instead of nailing them.

At noon we barely had enough fish to feed our six crew and three boatmen. To be precise, I had caught one small laker of about 2 lb, having pulled the hook out of a fair sized fish. So we motored over to a shallow bay, and while the guides got the fire going, we all had a spin from the shore to catch pike for lunch. And would you believe it, in this unknown bay not even fished by the guides, we took more than enough pike for shore lunch in 30 minutes than Nap and I could muster for the camera the day before from one of his favourite hot spots.

At 2.30 pm we finished lunch and by three o'clock with just three hours of the day left (everyone gets back to the dock for six) we arrived at Sugar Walls, a huge 100 acre bay so named due to its sheer sides where depth shelves down from six to over sixty feet, in as many feet out from the wooded shoreline. On one spot the fish finder recorded 103 feet, and as we made the first troll covering a large circle, several sizeable groups of trout came up on the screen. Within 20 minutes something grabbed the big spoon, but came unstuck half-way up. I decided to swap over from 15 lb test monofilament to 15 lb test low stretch dacron, and immediately this made all the difference. Even with the big chrome and orange spoon set at

70 feet, on the dacron I could feel the fish a little before Nap gunned the engine to help take up the slack. The first lake trout of respectable size weighed around 12 lb and gave both cameras some excellent footage. This was shortly followed by a thumping fish of around 16 lb. They were getting bigger.

Unfortunately, the time was whizzing by and there was less than an hour and a half of fishing left. On the next troll, just as we came around to the deepest part of the bay with the lure set at over 70 feet in 95 feet of water, the rod sprung back and I heaved back into what was obviously the big one we were all hoping for, as Nap gunned the motor to keep the line tight. Then the unexpected happened. The nine foot carbon trolling rod suddenly snapped off like a carrot a foot above the reel; but miraculously the fish was still on. Quickly Nap over-

lapped the two sections and held them tightly together, while I wound frantically, and for a minute or so I thought we were actually going to capture everything on both cameras. But the fish was gone, and we all relaxed in a wave of uncontrollable laughter. This meant a changeover, fixing the reel with the dacron onto another rod; we were certainly leaving it a bit tight. As a last resort I changed lures from the big spoon to a large rapala diving plug and for added attraction slipped a piece of fish skin (from the pike we had for shore lunch) over the size 6/0 single hook.

On the first complete troll of the bay I missed a slamming take. On the second, which we had all agreed was to be our last, we finally struck gold. The fish we had been waiting for hit the rapala and the rod bent into a nice full curve as deep down in over 70 feet of water a 20 lb plus laker battled away. After a spectacular five minute scrap it hit the surface in a flurry of spray, shaking its head like a dog with a bone. Nap bundled it into the net on the first attempt and we had it all in the can. Instantly I felt a wave of relief; the pressure of filming and leaving everything till the last moment is tremendous. That night we all slept soundly.

Thursday 26

Sunny all day. Slight wind.

In terms of producing the goods on film, today proved refreshingly relaxing. We took a boat up to the rapids close to the lodge and I caught a few pike while Paul shot underwater scenes. During the early evening we captured the sun going down through the trees while we shot a leaving scene with me doing a travelogue leaning up against a group of rocks on the beach. With the sun disappearing fast I had no time to fluff my lines and luckily it all went well.

Friday 27

Sunny all day. Gentle breeze.

This was our final day of fishing and filming on Nueltin Lake. The main objective being to complete some grayling fill-in sequences, we were all at the boat dock at 8 am sharp for the long trip up to the fourth narrows.

We beached the boats on the edge of a rocky island at a point where two fast flows converge; a real grayling hot spot if

Highlight of the day when out boat fishing Canada's huge lakes is stopping for shore lunch where your guide provides a sumptuous meal of fried pike, trout or grayling.

The Red River which runs through Winnipeg in the province of Manitoba is stuffed full of fish: walleye, sauger, white bass, bullheads and carp to over 40 lb. But Stu Mackay, my guide, had promised a lunker catfish.

ever there was one. I pulled into a beauty of 2¼ lb on the very first cast; it took a tiny spinner presented on the fly rod just as the lure was leaving the fast, turbulent main run and entering a deep pool. Several more grayling followed and then the inevitable happened – yes, a big laker sucked in the tiny inch-long lure and fair whizzed off into the turbulent main flow. It was a superb, thickset fish which led me a real song and dance for fully ten minutes before I had it under control and quiet enough to beach on a shallow sandy plateau. After several more grayling, all superb fish, including several over 2 lb, we wrapped, to make the long journey back in time for dinner, with more than enough grayling fill-in material in the can.

The fishing this past fortnight, though we were plagued by bad weather at first which lost us three precious days at Rankin Inlet, has been some of the most enjoyable I have known anywhere in the world. Tomorrow we film a few shots of the 748 Hawker Sidley coming in. This will then take us to Winnipeg where we have a full day's catfishing arranged at Lockport Dam on the Red River with Stu Mackay.

Sunday 29

Sunny all day. Very strong northerly wind.

We flew into Winnipeg from Nueltin yesterday evening without any hitches and had a good night's sleep ready for this morning's shoot, our last. Our location is the Red River at Lockport Bridge Dam on the outskirts of Winnipeg; a river which eventually feeds Lake Winnipeg, the fourteenth largest sheet of freshwater in the world, 260 miles long and up to 60 miles wide. The name Winnipeg in Cree Indian means muddy waters, and the Red River certainly lives up to its name as well. It has a strong flow, varies between 15 and 40 feet deep, and is over 200 yards wide below Lockport Dam. It is heavily coloured due to the red clay through which it runs, and simply full of fish. The species it contains are too numerous to name, but those most sought after are walleye and sauger (both similar to the European zander), white bass, goldeye, common carp in prolific numbers up to 40 lb, bullheads and the fish we came specifically to catch – the channel catfish. So numerous are channel catfish in the 15–30 lb range during the spring and fall that Lockport has deservedly been given the name of 'catfish capital of the world'.

Trouble was, no one told the catfish we were coming, and by 4 pm, having been as far as 20 miles downriver and back again, stopping at least six times (despite good concentrations of big cats showing on the electronic fish finder), all to no avail, we were getting a little worried. Was this going to be my first TV blank after completing the making of nearly 30 half hour programmes? Well fortunately, no! With an hour to spare, a bite was felt at last. The rod tip nodded a couple of times and the line tightened as I struck heavily – into thin air. I inspected the half inch thick steak cut from the middle of a freshly killed goldeye still neatly impaled on the chemically sharpened 1/0. It looked fine to me, but Stu pointed out the missing scales from the lower half where a cat had simply sucked at the bait and rejected it, possibly after having felt resistance from the rod tip. Channel cats are exceptionally sensitive to resistance and so on the next hit (it was, in fact, the second and last), I lowered the rod tip quickly after feeling the gentle knock of the bait being mouthed. After 30 seconds the line slowly tightened in a most positive way and I gave a hoot of joy when the rod took on a full, pulsating curve and kept there after a powerful strike. The cat stayed deep all the way to the boat, made several glorious, heavy, tail slapping dives and swirls alongside (all good stuff for the cameras), and then Stu had him in the net. A chunky fish of around 14 lb. So over the moon were we all after cracking it on our final shoot, that we forgot to weigh the cat.

After packing away all the equipment for our crew of six, a total of 27 pieces of luggage, and checking our flight times, we went out for a last evening meal in Winnipeg with Tom Dickie (who had run us around in his van) and Denis Maksymetz, both of Manitoba Tourism, plus Stu Mackay and Marvin Cooke, without whose help the catfishing would not have happened. Over a good bottle of champagne we toasted a successful two week shoot in Canada, even if it had been exceptionally tiring. We hit the sack at around midnight and enjoyed a well-earned lie-in until eight thirty the following morning. We then checked into Winnipeg International Airport for a two hour flight to Toronto, followed by a two hour wait for our long haul flight direct to Gatwick. *Go Fishing* 5 had two programmes in the bag already.

Misty dawn followed by clear skies and strong sunlight.

Just my luck that Britain should have been treated to a heatwave with day after day of temperatures in the nineties while we were in Canada; I figured I must have really missed out on the big carp in Warblers lake. So, this morning I woke to my alarm set for 3.15 in order to be in position and fishing a betalight float at the dam end before dawn broke. Everything was perfect. Within ten minutes a massive head and shoulders broke surface close to the bank beneath the trees where I had scattered a handful of American peanuts, mere feet from the luminous float tip. I was seconds away from a big one, but it never happened. Not even a line bite. Carp were certainly in the swim and feeding earnestly on the nuts for a good hour or more. I sat on the dry ground following the movements of individual carp through binoculars by observing their feeding bubbles spewing to the surface at regular intervals. It was a lesson in patience, and one of the few occasions when I have not been able to instigate at least one strikable bite.

After watching a very large rat feeding on discarded bait left in the margins, nattering with a friendly hedgehog and photographing a family of swans preening themselves in the burning sunshine, I left the lake happily at 8.30 am and headed the car towards Norwich glad just to be alive. Without blanks to put it all in perspective, especially after the ridiculously easy trout fishing I enjoyed in Canada last week, the good days can never be fully appreciated.

Wednesday 8

Humid and hazy. No wind.

Grass carp show a remarkable resemblance to chub and are often mistaken for them, but their eyes are set lower and the mouth is smaller.

This evening was so pleasant that I decided to have an hour's sport after grass carp at the bottom end of the new lake close to the house. There is not a huge stock of this unusual Asian fish, which looks more like a chub than a carp except that its mouth is noticeably smaller and its eyes are set much lower down. I introduced a couple of dozen between six ounces and two pounds a few years back, and considering they have to compete with a prolific stock of both king and wild carp, they have done exceptionally well. Earlier this summer saw the first caught into double figures, a beauty of 10¾ lb and this was followed just a week later by another

The only way of being selective when seeking grass carp is to present surface baits so that you can actually see which carp grabs hold. John offered a small cube of floating crust to this eight pounder.

of almost the same weight. As they are not able to reproduce in the wild in our climate, they are the ideal, controllable stock fish, which add a splash of variation to the carp, chub, eels and catfish which my syndicate members enjoy catching. They are an exceptionally timid feeder when competing with other species, particularly king and wild carp. Never do the grassies go around like a pot-bellied mirror, head and shoulders above the surface munching down floaters piece-meal. They slowly rise from directly beneath the bait and ever so gently suck it in, often momentarily pursing it between their lips before swallowing. Of course this means that striking quickly is suicidal. Occasionally someone catches a grass carp from the lakes on a bottom bait intended for carp – luncheon meat, peanuts, sweetcorn and the like – but of course these are completely chance catches. There is no way of being selective if you cannot see which fish takes the bait. So all in all, floater fishing, either freelining or using a small controller float, is the best method of approach if you only want to catch grass carp. And even then, up will pop a fat mirror and grab the floater off the grassy's nose just as it's about to suck it in. In fact this is exactly what happened to me this evening on the very first cast, having spotted a big grassy quietly sucking in floaters alongside a clump of white lilies. Luckily the hook pulled as it shot off in a huge furrow down the lake, and luckier still, the same grass carp plus a smaller fish were still periodically showing for the trout pellet feed I had scattered amongst the lilies. For hook bait however, I was presenting a small piece of brown crust on a size 10 tied direct to 6 lb test.

After easing the crust cube away from several obvious takers including a nice common, well into double figures, I managed softly to dunk it ahead of a grassy which took it immediately. It was the smaller of the two I could see, and all hell broke loose in the lilies. In addition to the grassy, there must have been a good dozen or so much bigger carp beneath the pads in water less than two feet deep, and they went berserk, shooting off in all directions. I actually felt on the line one bump into the grassy I was playing. It's a wonder the hook didn't pull out, such was the commotion. After a spirited fight, certainly as hard as I would have expected from any carp of the same size, the grassy tired and I slid it over the

waiting net. A lovely long fish of close on 8 lb. It was a beautifully conditioned specimen, like a torpedo, with not a scale out of place and it was exactly what I wanted to catch, having promised a publisher some grass carp transparencies. Living with water on your doorstep certainly does have its advantages.

With the weather pattern stable, I just couldn't resist another early morning session after the big carp of Warblers lake. The summer is marching on and I have yet to bank a carp from here anywhere near the size of which the lake is capable of producing. The alarm was set for

9 **Thursday**

Sunny all day and very warm.

115

3.30 am, but I must have been tired and dozed off again, only to wake suddenly at 4.30 am with dawn about to break and a 30 minute drive ahead. I popped my head out of the bedroom window and decided to go anyway, despite missing out on that all-important pre-dawn period.

Only a few patches of stale bubbles were visible on the surface at the dam end when I arrived, still well before sun-up. It seemed the carp had not been as active as the weather suggested, but I settled beneath the overhanging chestnut, nonetheless, scattered a few jumbo peanuts and followed in with two on a size 4 and a lift float rig. I also scattered in two handfuls of mixed tares and hempseed which soon had the tench at least, rooting the bottom up. I even hooked one of about 2 lb which took a liking for the double peanuts to 11 lb line. Fortunately it came off, and so the area was not unduly disturbed.

For a couple of hours very little happened apart from several tench fizzing away in the swim. I flicked peanuts to a family of mice which kept disappearing with them, no doubt to be stored, and I sat fascinated for a while watching the same family of swans that I photographed not long back. The six cygnets are now growing up fast and were being taught how to wash and preen their wings by the pen, while the cob watched masterfully from afar. In an undulating movement, starting with her long neck thrust beneath the surface, the pen forced water over her wings by partly submerging them. Immediately afterwards a long preening session commenced with all the cygnets following suit. All this took place in the middle of the lake where thick weed beds reach almost to the surface. They are so thick that when carp move along the dam end, they swim over the top with their backs, dorsals and tail well above the waterline. They then sink down again as they patrol the weed-free margins shaded from direct sunlight by tall overhanging willows and the chestnuts beneath which I generally sit.

When the swans departed, a lone fish which I followed through binoculars for a good 50 yards as it came over the weed beds down the middle of the lake, made a beeline for the swim. I clearly saw the immense width across its shoulders as it humped over the weed bed towards me not five yards beyond the float tip. The surface smoothed over when it dived down and for fully 10 seconds nothing happened. Then two things occurred simultaneously; the float sunk positively and the rod, which was lying on the grass with the tip just beyond the margins, lurched forwards violently. Instinctively I grabbed and lifted the 12 foot carbon into a full curve against the huge fish which was now half way across the lake taking line against a screaming clutch. In several unstoppable surges it reached the margins some 80 yards away along the opposite bank, where thick sedges hung out into the shallows, and veered to the left. By now I had disentangled the rod tip from the branches of the overhanging chestnut and was starting to count my chickens. It was certainly 25 lb plus and in all probability that 30 pounder I had been after for the last three seasons. Then, quite gently, as if to teach me a lesson, the hook slipped out. On inspection, the well-sharpened point was burred over as if it had hit bone or a scale. But the fish certainly didn't feel foulhooked. Who really knows? Only the carp.

E ven though I held a rod for less than three minutes, today's fishing was a memorable experience, putting me back in touch with some of the fundamentals of life and sport. Forsaking Norfolk, Tania and I drove down to South Cerney, near Cirencester in Gloucestershire where the National Coarse Fishing Festival for the Disabled was being held on the huge gravel pit complex controlled by the South Cerney Angling Club. Organised for the last nine years by Brian Sefton, vice chairman of the South Cerney Club, this is the largest competition solely for disabled anglers anywhere in Europe – possibly in the world – and last year attracted a staggering 300 contestants.

Brian and his team who, in addition to laying on prizes, provide a steady supply of soft drinks and beer throughout the match with the compliments of local traders, invited me along last August to present the prizes to the juniors. This year over 400 handicapped anglers from all over the U.K. and from every walk of life, cast out their lines when the whistle was blown at 11 am to start the match in bright sunshine and

14 Sunday

Hot and sunny all day.

The National Coarse Fishing Festival for the Disabled, hosted yearly by the South Cerney Fishing Club near Cirencester in Gloucestershire, attracts anglers of all ages and disabilities. A lack of arms doesn't stop Tony Jarvis from Wolverhampton catching roach on the waggler; he uses a closed face reel operated by his big toe.

soaring temperatures. In the company of old friends Peter and Doreen Williams who first made me aware that this event existed and talked me into attending, we all felt exhausted simply walking around watching the contestants who, despite the heatwave conditions, found tench and small roach close in during the first hour and during the last.

A local company were producing a video of the event and asked if I would interview some of the contestants, which I was only too pleased to do. Seeing anglers who are physically and or mentally handicapped, and so much worse off than the rest of us, enjoying their sport without a moan between them was indeed an inspiring sight. One particularly cheerful contestant, Tony Jarvis from near Wolverhampton, caught my attention. Despite having no arms, Tony was putting a

waggler out some 20 yards over his head as straight as an arrow into 10 feet of water, sinking the line to counteract the waves and wind drift, and taking small roach on a single red maggot to a size 22 hook. How, you may well ask? By having the handle of his 13 foot carbon float rod strapped to his left (casting) foot. The reel being a closed face, fixed upside down on the handle, allowed Tony's right big toe to depress the casting button. He then brought his toes into action for winding, all in one very smooth, quick movement. Far smoother than most fishermen blessed with arms, I can tell you. Some sat in wheel-chairs, some were lying down; some had loved ones to assist, some did everything for themselves. The event, just as it did last year, left me feeling very humble and content with my own good fortune.

Above left: Perhaps better known for the money he raises for disabled people by sponsored wheelchair rides, Robbie Robertson is also a dab hand at catching tench on the pole.

Above right: The final weight of Robbie's catch – over 15 lb – made 3rd prize in the South Cerney Festival which attracted over 400 anglers.

119

We spent the last half hour before the final whistle sitting behind Robbie Robertson's wheel-chair. Robbie, who recently made the Guinness Book of Records with the quickest wheelchair ride in the U.K. from John O'Groats to Lands End, raising £21,000 for disabled people in the process, looked as though he was way out in front. Although the tench had not started fizzing in his weedy six foot deep swim till 1 pm, he quickly put six in the keep net on the pole before a big one snapped the end rig. He quickly made up a waggler outfit for the last ten minutes, but had to settle for third place overall with a creditable 15 lb catch. However he did come first in the wheelchair section. When the final whistle went at 3 pm, I could not resist it any longer and asked Robbie for a cast with his rod which resulted in a bite and a tench on straight away. I then promptly went and lost it 30 seconds later in the weeds, to hoots of laughter from the onlookers and scalesmen waiting to weigh in Robbie's catch, not to mention Tania, Pete and Doreen.

Then it was all back to the huge marquee for a nosh and the final, very moving event of the day – the prize giving. As last year, I was introduced to present all the juniors with their prizes (they all get one whether they catch anything or not). It was wonderful and a tribute to everyone involved with the festival. Standing there holding a trophy or tackle prize waiting for the youngster to battle his way over on crutches or in a wheel-chair, I fought hard, just as I had to last year, to bite back the tears choking my throat; not from pity, because that's not what it's about, but from joy. What a truly wonderful day it had been; by far the most emotional occasion connected with fishing that I have ever experienced. There's no doubt about it, they'll have to fight to stop me coming back again next August.

Wednesday 22

Humid, bright sunshine all day.

I realised that I had not fished my local River Wensum for months, even though it winds its way through a beautiful valley not 200 yards from the house. Not since the end of the season in fact, just before I set off for India. That's the trouble with leading a busy fishing life which this year has

included visiting a number of foreign locations, in order to both research and make television programmes. This morning I decided to put things right and picked up Charlie Clay at 5 am, as dawn was about to break. After loading all Charlie's tackle (it was *supposed* to be a wandering session) into the back of the car, there was just a short drive along bumpy lanes down to the river at Lyng where the Norfolk Anglers Conservation Association controls a lovely fast, shallow and heavily overgrown stretch, full of chub – our morning's quarry.

My immediate impression was how the days are already drawing in after the consistent hot weather this summer; this year's winter will need to be particularly wet if the underground aquifers are to be replenished with the water taken by the continuing drought.

Because it was dry, we failed to gather any slugs or worms and so relied for bait upon a fresh white loaf and a handful of floating plugs including Ryobi muggers, little S, and crazy crawlers. I simply love the fun that can be had working out chub from where they lie beneath rafts of cut weed or marginal watercress mats, up onto the surface. I once took eight chub on plugs from the river in a mad two hour session, all between 2½ and 4 lb on a big S plug which the majority of

What beauty summer chub fishing has to offer. Flanked by tall beds of Himalayan balsam and a profusion of subtle colours, Charlie Clay eases a nice chub over the gravel shallows towards the net. Using surface plugs and freelined breadflake, Charlie and I took 15 chub during a morning's stint on the River Wensum at Lyng.

anglers would never credit a chub attacking. The truth is that next to pike and trout, chub are the most voracious predators in the river, consuming fish fry from a very early age. Once mature they also fall readily for floating divers gurgled and spluttered over the trailing weed beds.

Conditions on the river were absolutely perfect. Despite the drought, the level seemed surprisingly high (probably the mill downriver was backing the flow up) and the water was crystal clear. When the piece of freelined flake hit the surface alongside an old overhanging willow, I first saw the furrow across the surface towards it, and then every scale on the 3 lb chub which sucked it confidently in with those huge rubbery lips. Because each scrap caused such a ridiculous commotion in the calm, clear conditions, tactics were very much of a hit

and run nature, swapping freelining gear every so often for my short single-handed American bait casting rod and baby multiplier, a lovely outfit to use for surface popping.

Once the sun was high above the trees, as usual everything did a disappearing act; someone walking the same winding two mile stretch at 10 am could easily believe not one chub existed in this part of the Wensum. But that's the secret of enjoying a wandering summer session after chub; for the very best sport you rise early and leave early.

In less than four hours (much of this time spent with the camera), we smelt the true delight of summer and marvelled at the wonderful display of Himalayan balsam which covered the margins with its white and pink flowers. We had repeatedly seen several kingfishers, dab chicks, numerous assorted ducks, a pair of swans, and rabbits by the hundred scampering across the flood plains as we meandered along. Oh, and not to forget part of the reason we came in the first place, Charlie took six and I accounted for nine chub, the best going on 3¾ lb. I felt guilty for having forgotten my beloved Wensum for so long.

Some of our fish came immediately downstream from specially constructed gravel riffles which N.A.C.A. working parties had put in during the close season. It's all part of a development plan based around this particular stretch which intends to re-establish definite features within the river to help breeding and create habitats. Their hard work is obviously paying dividends.

On the way back to the house I asked Charlie if he minded stopping in Lenwade at the common pits, because there was a photography sequence I wanted to shoot for a book I am preparing. In theory taking a few before and after shots of cleaning a swim out with a weed drag should have been simple. It was a nice sunny day and the margins were covered in the beautiful yellow dwarf pond lily. However half-way through (Charlie of course did the dragging – I'm not as silly as I look) the drag became stuck fast on the bottom; probably snagged on an old tree stump. One way out would have been to go home and fetch the boat. On the other hand the quick and easy way was to strip off to my underpants and remove it in person which, after the initial shock of cold water, was wonderfully refreshing.

Another one for Charlie. Stalking stealthily is the essence of fooling the chub inhabiting the clear running water of the river during the summer months. Creep up quietly so that they are unaware of your presence and they can readily be taken from almost beneath the rod tip. Note the flick up, telescopic, trout-type landing net which clips onto the waistcoat when not in use.

Friday 7

Overcast with scattered heavy showers all day. Gale force winds.

Having seen a particularly long fish beneath the raft we were both fishing, I mentioned to 'Veg' (Kevin Gardner) that his first barbel from the Wensum might well be a double. It was – all 12 lb 2 oz of it.

In the pouring rain, I net my second eight pounder which, like the first, sucked up two small meat cubes, hair rigged on a size 8 tied direct to 6 lb test.

This, I thought when the digital alarm emitted its nauseating bleep, was not the morning to go barbel hunting along the Wensum Valley, even if it was close to home. I could hear the wind crashing the branches of the tall birch and oaks next to the house and the drumming of heavy rain against the window panes. Why I had arranged to meet 'Veg' (Kevin Gardner) down by the mill at Costessey at the unearthly hour of 5 am, heaven only knows. If it were not for the fact that Veg had never caught a barbel – the main reason for organising the session – I would have turned over and returned to the land of nod. But then, quite suddenly, that old buoyant feeling was there, teeth were brushed and I was in the car, trundling along the Fakenham Road flattening the twigs and small branches deposited by the wind during the night. Not a rabbit could be seen.

I was rather worried that I might be late for our rendezvous, but Veg was not there anyway, and it was still dark. After warming myself for a few minutes by turning the heater up full blast with the engine going, I took the torch and illuminated the shallow water pouring through the middle sluice. It held nothing but minnows in an even depth of just six inches, where once there was up to four feet of water. I also shone the torch into the main mill pool, hardly flowing due to the lack of rain over the past two months and not exactly helped by the installation two years back of a dreaded 'pressure plate weir'. There was not a fish to be seen. There was rain, and plenty of it. As I unpacked the tackle from the car with dawn breaking, wondering what had happened to Veg, the heavens opened. But it was short-lived and I was soon on my way across the meadows to a favourite old barbel swim; a long line of overhanging willows on the opposite bank where a huge raft of debris collects, forming a dark cavern over the gravel run beneath.

However, when I reached the swim the heavens opened yet again and I was completely soaked through within minutes – served me right for not bothering to take waterproofs along. And that is more or less what happened till I left the river for my shop in Norwich at 8.30 am, heavy rain on and off the whole time. Not that I really cared, because within minutes of scattering a pint of hemp plus a handful of luncheon meat cubes into the head of the swim, several good barbel and chub

moved out from beneath the raft to wolf it up. Being a popular swim fished regularly from both banks by a number of barbel enthusiasts, the occupants know all about hemp seed and luncheon meat. Yet they still feed on this magical combination most willingly. I sleeved two small cubes of meat onto a ¾" hair tied to a size 8 direct on 6 lb test, and with four swan shots on a link to hold bottom in the strong flow, plopped it close to the raft on the opposite bank so the meat settled where I could keep a watchful eye on it, just a foot out from the shadow of the debris above.

Not five minutes elapsed, during which time several chub and a group of five nice bream passed over the bait heading upstream, when a lone barbel suddenly slipped out from beneath the raft and grabbed the meat. I struck instantly and scrambled a few yards downriver to get below the fish, keeping the rod tip low to the water as it powered under the willows, pulling the 12 foot 1¼ lb test Avon into an alarming curve. I could feel its tail clanging against sub-surface branches, yet miraculously the fish kited upstream against the pressure of side strain without the line or the swan shot link fouling. Accompanied by another downpour, the barbel was now mid-river, charging along the bottom through clumps of soft blanket and streamer weeds well clear of the raft and well out of harm's way. After a couple of heavy swirls on the surface and much chugging about below and above the raft, it characteristically rolled on the top, completely knackered, and came straight to the net. By this time I was of course even wetter, but better off to the tune of a lovely long Wensum barbel tipping the scales down to 8 lb 6 oz. After unhooking it quickly and soaking the giant micro-mesh keep net which I staked out 20 yards upstream where the current ran fast close in to the bank, I popped the barbel in and was pleased to see it turn immediately around with its head into the flow.

As I scrambled back up the high banking, there was Veg clutching a bunch of rods, hurrying across the long grass towards me muttering apologies about useless alarm clocks. I related the series of events and assured him that if we sat together side by side and both fished the same swim, his chance of achieving a personal ambition and hooking into a barbel was definitely on the cards. So once Veg had set up a similar rig on his quiver tip rod and put in a few more handfuls of hemp we crept into the swim and waited, with both our hook baits just five feet apart immediately below the shadow of the raft. With this kind of visual fishing in a confined area, rod rests become obsolete and so holding the rod for a quick strike and immediate control of a fish is imperative, or a lost whopper could result. Every so often a good barbel would spin itself over, as they do, along the bottom to disturb the gravel and dislodge particles of food – natural food like shrimps and, of course, the hemp seed and tiny cubes of luncheon meat. Fortunately they really were in an aggressive feeding mood, and it was not long after a few near misses, with barbel refusing our baits at the last moment (it's great watching them doing this) before another found itself hooked. It was a fish I had been watching closely for some time, moving about at the upstream end of the run, returning from beneath the raft, picking up a few food particles and quickly slipping back in again. Only on this occasion as it departed, so had my cubes of meat and an impulse strike saw the barbel's tail lash heavily as it powered beneath the raft, well and truly hooked. Veg very quickly reeled in as I scrambled over his feet to get below the fish with the rod tip low to the water. Like the first fish, it too had designs on those snags and I was not about to allow it sanctuary, though for a good thirty seconds I could do little except keep applying heavy side strain and simply hang on, hoping the six pound test held. After almost a carbon copy of the previous fight, even down to the route taken by the first barbel, I had it in the net inside a couple of minutes. At 8 lb 5 oz it was not far short of being an identical size either.

The time was now just after 8.15 am and after Veg had taken a few photos, I gathered my gear ready to head for work. I vividly remember saying to Veg, who by now must have thought the gods were really shining down upon me, that I would not be at all surprised if his first barbel, as for so many other anglers trying the Wensum, was a double figure fish. We had, in fact, seen a really long (obvious double) fish moving beneath the raft before I hooked into the second. So I left Veg sitting there in the rain, but in hope.

At around 10.30 am I answered the telephone. It was a breathless Veg: 'Guess what I've just caught' he said, 'a 12 lb 2 oz barbel'. There was a real sense of incredulity in his voice, but I, for one, was not the slightest bit surprised. Naturally, Veg wanted someone to take a few pics, and as luck would have it, Simon Earp, who has used my Bronica before, was in the shop buying some tackle. He was, of course, only too pleased, to oblige as fishing mates always are. Well done Veg!

LAND OF THE VIKINGS

Friday 14

Martin Founds shows the variety of quality fish living in Denmark's fabulous River Guden: beautifully coloured rudd to over 2 lb, bronze-backed bream and mountains of roach just waiting to grab the bait in every swim. Whether quiver tipping or long-trotting the streamy runs, that old saying of 'a bite a chuck' comes true here.

Second cameraman, Ron Tufnell, who also lives in Norfolk, was round at the house three minutes early, followed by Martin Founds, whose Range Rover crunched along the gravel drive at exactly 12 noon after a three hour drive from Chesterfield in Derbyshire. Yet another *Go Fishing* programme for Anglia Television, this time to be filmed in Denmark, was underway. After loading up all the tackle, we drove to Harwich to rendezvous with the rest of the crew and catch the five o'clock Scandinavian Seaways Ferry to Esbjerg on the west coast – Denmark's largest fishing port.

Denmark is, in fact, a collection of some 500 islands with its three largest land masses situated quite close together. Connected to the northern tip of Germany is Jutland, the Danish mainland. Funen lies to its west and is connected by road, while Sealand is just a short ferry trip away to the west and boasts the capital, Copenhagen. Denmark is not blessed with 100,000 deep water lakes like its westerly neighbour, Sweden, but those it does contain are simply full of fish, and bisected by some fabulous river systems. The lakelands around Silkeborg were our chosen location for *Go Fishing*; an area not unlike the Norfolk Broads, only with far, far fewer boats. The famous River Guden, Denmark's longest river, enters the lakes at Silkeborg from the south east and after flowing through the middle, leaves from the north-western shoreline to flow north-east in the direction of Randers, finally spewing its waters through a fiord into the Baltic Sea.

My old mates, Dave Thomas from Leeds, Terry Smith, fellow tackle dealer and rod builder from Sheffield and Keith Lidgett from Lincoln were, I am glad to say, included amongst the party. Having visited Denmark regularly in a research capacity for *Anglers World Holidays*, their combined knowledge of this fascinating lakeland and river system is second to none. And I felt in the very best of hands. That was until we arrived at Harwich to find that director/cameraman, Paul Martingel and sound recordist Dave Lindsay had yet to arrive with all the filming equipment, and Terry Smith's Volkswagen van, carrying all the fishing tackle and baits, was stuck in 3rd gear. Not exactly the best of omens, but then I am neither superstitious nor a fatalist, and within an hour we

were all on board, along with Melissa Robertson the production assistant and Dave Farrant of Scandinavian Seaways, who kindly arranged the crossings. Paul and Dave had made the customs hall and the ramp by the skin of their teeth. Their vehicle was, in fact, the very last on. For anyone wishing to travel to Denmark via Scandinavian Seaways, I can thoroughly recommend the facilities available on board during the 20 hour voyage. With the famous hot and cold buffet tables, the cinemas, discos and excellent cabaret, the trip is more like a mini cruise than a ferry. It was wonderful for us all to be able to relax and to structure how we thought the programme might go, although with fishing, which is always based on a certain degree of luck, you can only plan so far.

We docked in Esbjerg at 1.30 pm on Saturday and within a short space of time, were through Danish customs and on our way towards Ry near Silkeborg, just 40 miles north east of Esbjerg.

It is refreshing to report that the uncluttered roads (just as well since Martin had to tow Terry's van most of the way) and easy pace of life make Denmark the ideal holiday resort for those touring or fishing. In point of fact, though it is about the size of England, Denmark contains less than half the population of London; just five million people. We finally arrived at the Ry Park Hotel at around 4 pm and took a quick stroll through the town beside the nearby River Guden which flows beneath a picturesque bridge and weir system, before sorting out the mountain of gear and changing for dinner.

Sunday 16

Warm, bright sunshine all day.
Gentle breeze.

With the sun already shining down from a blue, cloudless sky, we started the first day's filming at Resenbro where the Guden meanders peacefully through picturesque farmlands, bordered on both banks by beds of bullrush, tall reeds and sedges. The river is not dissimilar to my local River Wensum in Norfolk; it varies between eight and fifteen yards wide, is quite clear, but has a noticeably quicker pace, with depths varying between two and six feet. It is full of character with numerous bends, bays and eddies, and simply full of fish, particularly roach and perch. I literally could not stop catching them. Though the roach would have been more readily taken by trotting down with a stick float, I decided to keep the bait on the bottom, hoping to contact the famous hard-fighting Guden bream. For this reason I opted to stret peg using a waggler fixed top and bottom and set well over depth with a mini two swan shot ledger stopped 12 inches above a size 10 hook. Bait was varied between bunches of four or five maggots, worms and sweetcorn, but I was continually plagued by roach and perch up to around the eight ounce stamp. If anyone wishes simply to see their float go down, this is the place, I can assure you.

After shooting some pretty introductions to the programme plus a look at the best way of transporting maggots by car and ferry (they are virtually unobtainable in Denmark), we decided to leave the stret pegging swim at lunchtime and move downriver to where Keith Lidgett had taken a few bream during the early morning. Keith was fishing with local expert Kaj Pederson (five times Danish freshwater champion) who had arranged for us to film on this lovely part of the Guden, and their swims, both with huge slacks on the opposite bank and fast water on the inside, were known bream hot spots. However, neither had taken bream since the sun had intensified, and I must admit to thinking that the chances of any more showing were rather remote. Nevertheless, I decided to move into a narrow gap in the tall reeds right at the upstream end of this stretch, just above Keith, and put in a helping of cereal feed laced with corn and casters; a deadly bream groundbait, if ever there was one, and hey presto, I got stuck into a modest bream of around 3 lb within half an hour. Bites came readily to quiver tipped corn or worm and corn cocktails, although for the first hour following the bream I was continually pestered with small perch and roach. The rig was a simple fixed paternoster with a size 10 hook and an ounce bomb (on a 6″ link) to keep the bait over the far side just on the edge of the slack. By using a long telescopic rod rest and angling the quiver tip rod almost vertically in the air, most of the line was kept off the surface, and the bait remained static. Obviously this was just what those bream wanted; if it moved, they simply weren't interested.

Right: Guden bream readily accept baits like breadflake, sweetcorn, maggots and worms. The larger specimens often show a distinct preference for a bunch of red maggots.

Facing page, top: About to hand out a Danish lakeland bream is ex-world champion Dave Thomas from Leeds. Dave regularly takes the Scandinavian Seaways Ferry across from Harwich to Esbjerg.

Right: A heavily reed-fringed lake close to Silkeborg, through which the River Guden flows, was one of the locations chosen for the Go Fishing programmes. In just five hours' filming it produced this 150 lb catch of bream, perch, rudd, roach and hybrids.

Facing page, below: Apart from fish in profusion, those who visit Denmark can enjoy many picturesque spots such as this beautiful pool in the River Guden, below the road bridge at Ry.

During the last hour of the day I managed another two bream, both around 3 lb. Not a brilliant start to the programme, but lots of nice intro shots and some interesting action. Having baited the swim heavily after packing up, the plan was for everyone to rise early in the morning and visit the same spot to try for the bream again.

Monday 17

Misty start, followed by intermittent cloud and sun all day.

For a change we decided to start filming very early in the morning, to show the beauty of the sun rising above the mist and why it is that fishermen set their alarm clocks for the dark hours. Unfortunately, bream in the kind of numbers I had anticipated, especially after heavily prebaiting the opposite bank slack at Resenbro, did not show. Terry Smith and I took perhaps a dozen up to 4 lb between us, plus some clonking great rudd to well over 2 lb. As is often the case on the Guden, there was no sure method of consistently getting through the massive roach shoals to the bigger fish, despite going up to a size 8 hook holding five corn kernels tied direct to a 4 lb hook link. Suddenly a bream would be there, followed by another batch of roach or perch, and then another bream, and so on. In retrospect I cannot believe the swims held enormous concentrations of bream because with the amount of bait we were putting in, both loose feed and cereal groundbait, I am sure they would have got their heads down at some time during the day.

Nevertheless, it was all wonderful action for the cameras, and as the sun decided to slip out from between the light cloud cover for much of the day, we could not have asked for better conditions. From the filming aspect, results look so much nicer when shot in sunshine. I am of the opinion that a fishing programme showing small fish, but with everything bathed in natural sunlight, is actually more appealing to the viewer than watching large fish caught in the pouring rain when a grey cloak hides the beauty of the countryside.

After lunch we wrapped the filming at Resenbro with more than enough on quiver tipping in the can, allowing most of the party to reconnoitre the large lakes near Silkeborg. This meant that Terry and I could carry on trying for the bream;

but inevitably the roach had other ideas. Whatever we threw at them be it maggots, casters, worms, corn or breadflake, a plump roach located it before the bream had a chance. What a prolific river the Guden is, I have never before experienced so many roach willing to feed all day long. Though we did not weigh our catches, the combined weight was well in excess of 100 lb and those roach were still pulling the quiver tip round when we packed up. For me the day was particularly enjoyable as it was ideal for shooting lots of stills (I got through nine rolls) on the Bronica ETRS, with fish coming out regularly in lovely sunshine and beautiful surroundings. The River Guden really is the closest I have ever seen in real life to those lovely Bernard Venables paintings of the 1950s *Mr. Crabtree* cartoons. His illustrations of winding, tree-clad rivers, so full of character and promise, motivated an entire generation of fishermen, yours truly included.

Having completed two sections of the programme on the River Guden, we decided that for variety, waggler fishing a typical reed-fringed Danish lake for bream would perhaps give the viewer and any future visitor to Denmark, an accurate account of the superb coarse fishing available. Terry Smith immediately suggested a lake in the suburbs of Silkeborg where, with enough cereal feed introduced early in the morning, it would be possible to keep the bream coming all day long. How right he was. So, it was a 6 am start yet again for Terry and I to sort out a suitable swim with good camera angles, so that hopefully, by the time the film crew arrived, it would be full of feeding bream. It is characteristic of most Danish lakes that they start very shallow at the edges and slowly shelve off. So in order to float fish effectively you need to don waders and walk out several yards until parallel with the reedline and then present the bait three to four rod lengths out in anywhere between five to eight feet of water. The lake at Silkeborg through which, incidentally, the River Guden flows, was no exception. It could not possibly have been fished from the shore-line due to

18 Tuesday

Cloudy start followed by strong sunlight all day.

an enormously thick marginal growth of tall common reed and marsh willows. Nevertheless it was a very picturesque spot indeed, with a good colour to the water, and unbelievably prolific in bream, mostly in the 2–3 lb range.

Fishing adjoining swims, Terry and I must have taken a good 20 bream apiece before the crew arrived, keeping the massive shoal interested with regular helpings of loose fed maggots and corn, plus balls of cereal laced with casters. It may sound crude, but five maggots on a size 10 hook tied direct to 4 lb reel line was very much the order of the day. A step down to smaller hooks only increases the chances of hooking roach or perch, both of which are only too quick to gobble the maggots up should the bream be slow to find them. Every so often a pound plus rudd or a roach/rudd hybrid would turn up to make things interesting, and I even landed a five pound pike which grabbed a small roach on the way in. In short, had I carried on all day, the net would have burst. As it was, we wrapped filming at 1 pm with more than enough material on tape (we use Betacam SB video cameras incidentally) all in glorious sunshine, and I still accounted for around 150 lb.

For once it was lovely to start shooting a sequence knowing that barring accidents (like a roach or perch grabbing the bait on the drop) the two swan peacock waggler would slowly sink beneath the surface and I would wind the 13 foot carbon into a lovely full curve and get another bream – not just occasionally, but cast after cast after cast. I have never experienced such frantic fishing for bream before, there seemed to be an endless supply of them. This just about sums up the lakeland fishing in Denmark; it is ridiculously prolific provided you follow the golden guideline: put in enough feed initially to attract the bream, and then keep it going in regularly to hold them. I am sure the pike fishing potential is tremendous with such a rich larder of shoal fish for them to feed upon, but sadly time prevented me from any exploration, that will have to wait for another day. As with most shoots, and despite the fact that the weather had been kind, we had precious little free time before packing everything up and driving back to Esbjerg for the return ferry trip to Harwich. Incidentally, fishing licences are available from all Danish tourist offices and you don't need an international driving licence, although green card insurance is, of course, compulsory. The most consistent period for sport is between May and October, and for a week's fishing you would need the following bait supply: a 56 lb sack of breadcrumbs; two gallons of maggots; two gallons of casters plus bags of corn, and at least a dozen tubs of worms. Bread can be purchased locally but it is not as doughy and therefore does not stay on the hook as well as the average UK white loaf.

30 Sunday

Overcast, intermittent rain all day.

I always obtain far more enjoyment from watching others achieve their dream catch than from hooking into biggies myself. I like recording the action through the camera lens and with youngsters especially, the look of wonder and pride on their smiling faces is always super to behold. Such was my enjoyment today, reeling off lots of film whilst Tania's fifteen year old nephew, Alex, battled with the carp. I would love to say that it was only yesterday when I first took Alex's dad Jonathan (Tania's brother) fishing, but I would be lying to the tune of around 25 years. Jonathan went under sufferance in those days and can only ever remember falling in and spending the night freezing cold in my fishing wagon, then an old A35 van. But his son Alex is made of much keener stuff and was looking forward to his first taste of carp fishing.

Tania had invited Jonathan, his wife Carol and their three children up to Norfolk to stay with us for the weekend and virtually promised Alex he could fulfil an ambition (with my help). How could I not oblige, although I must admit for quite some time the thought did cross my mind that he might log up a blank considering the dour, overcast day. With showers of intermittent rain which saw us all (the whole family had to come and watch) scampering back indoors, producing carp to order from the lakes, well stocked as they are, proved, until just before lunch, almost impossible. Then a carp popped up and sucked down the floater confidently enough for young Alex to strike and bang the hook home. Until then those he struck at stood little chance of being hooked due to an excess of slack line. There was a slight draw on the surface and as the floater drifted inwards, initially Alex

Travelling the 100 miles from Hertfordshire up to Norfolk to fish my lakes for the day gave young Alex Sheath precious little fishing time. Nevertheless, he accounted for a brace of mirror carp to 11 lb.

could not get the hang of mending the line continually, to keep in check with the bait. Unfortunately, just as Tania was about to net Alex's first carp, a small common of around 3 lb, the hook suddenly fell out. Obviously it was never really home in the first place. Not to be outdone, on went another floater and with continuous badgering from yours truly about not allowing the line to belly, suddenly Alex's rod bent double and the clutch screamed as a fish sped away. This time he wasn't taking any prisoners and the hook held till Tania slid the net beneath his first ever carp, and a nice one too, a plump mirror of about 9 lb. Alex was over the moon. By now Wilson was almost drained; it's surprising how much nervous energy you can use up simply helping another to catch fish, and so we called a halt for lunch up at the local pub.

Late in the afternoon following a further two hours of frustration, intermittent squally showers, ruined chances and carp which were in no way cooperative, quite suddenly Alex was in again, and this time a nice fish obviously into double figures had also succumbed to floaters. It gave him an exciting tussle for several minutes in and around the lily beds, before it was ready for the net. Another mirror of 11 lb exactly. I rather think that there was at least one happy teenager on the drive back to Hertfordshire when Jonathan and Carol packed up all the gear and set off as darkness quickly fell over the lakes. It had been a rather nostalgic day for me and, as always, lovely to see sizeable fish taken by a youngster.

Thursday 4

Clear skies, windy day followed by a mild evening.

In addition to being a fellow angling writer, my good friend Dave Batten from Watton is also an accomplished illustrator of fishing books. And since he was coming round this evening to discuss the line drawings for a series of coarse fishing books I am writing, we thought a couple of hours carp fishing first would be rather nice.

We planned to meet at the house when I returned home from work at around 6 pm and to fish adjoining swims in the small lake where we could also have a good old natter. Friends Mike and Heather Clowser from Kings Lynn, who had been carp fishing all day and accounted for no less than

19 fish up to 12 lb between them (nearly all mirrors), had already packed their rods away when Dave and I arrived, and were about to open the customary bottle of red wine. It is a relaxing ritual which Mike and Heather invariably enjoy following a successful day's sport; so, forced by tradition, Dave and I obligingly settled down on our stools beneath the canopy of white willows and silver birches, reluctantly had our paper cups filled, and for some time did our best to put the world right. Naturally, we didn't have any solutions and so after a while another bottle was opened. Fortunately, Dave and I had scattered in a pint of hemp seed plus luncheon meat cubes before our happy hour started, and now having discussed the trials of life, the Middle East crisis and the escalating price of maggots we were feeling slightly the worse for wear. With darkness approaching we fitted starlight luminous elements to the tips of our lift rigs and reluctantly started fishing, bidding Mike and Heather a fond farewell.

I don't know about Dave, because a large alder separated us, but I found concentration extremely difficult and completely missed the first bite, the float disappearing as though the carp had really meant business. But I didn't miss the second a few minutes later, and as the peacock quill lifted positively and was on the point of toppling over, I whacked the 12 foot carbon Avon back and really banged the size 8 home with perhaps rather more force than necessary for 6 lb test. The carp quickly veered to the left away from the four foot deep bar where it sucked up the luncheon meat, going straight through Dave's swim and over the marginal drop, off into deeper water. For a carp which turned out to weigh a shade over 10 lb it really ripped off a lot of line and put up a formidable scrap. Isn't it strange that fish always feel much larger than they are when hooked in the dark? Perhaps it is because we cannot see the way the rod is bending, or the fact that our imagination runs wild. Either way, it was still a lovely deep-set common carp in mint condition. Half an hour later I hooked another which slipped the hook after belting off half-way across the lake, and shortly afterwards suffered an almost identical performance. Meanwhile, Dave's swim had been void of carp till he missed a sailaway bite just before we agreed to wrap at 9 pm, and get on with our publishing work back at the house. What a lovely evening.

*Typical autumn day – windy,
with intermittent patches of
cloud and sunshine.*

Had we not been out to dinner with friends Norman and Vera Symmonds, who own the Homersfield Lake carp fishery near Bungay in Suffolk, and hit the sack late, and had my subsequent headache not been so unbearable, Tania and I would perhaps have set off pike fishing a good deal earlier, as planned. As it was, we finally arrived at the Conifers lake (where my son Lee boated a near 24 pounder way back in January) for the first pike assault of this winter, definitely the wrong side of 10 am. To make matters even worse, the boat (the only boat available) was out of the water for its annual paint job and a couple of new boards.

As the 15 acre lake is surrounded by heavy reedlines and mature trees, with next to no bank fishing space except for the wooden staging adjacent to the boat house, there was no argument as to where the pike were going or not going to be caught. Usually when I fish this enchanting lake, which averages between 10 to 15 feet deep away from the shoreline, it is from the boat anchored across the wind, which affords a wide area in which to work both drifted and static deadbaits plus artificial lures. Consequently I felt at a distinct disadvantage having only the one spot to show Tania the excitement of pike fishing. In addition, the water was the clearest I have ever seen it. Usually until a few heavy frosts kill off the phytoplankton, the lake throughout the summer and autumn is a thick pea green with only minimal visibility. Yet today, mussel shells littering the bottom could clearly be seen through ten feet of water only a few feet out from the staging. So could shoals of young roach and perch. It would appear that we were literally standing above their food supply. Twice as I feverishly rigged up a couple of rods, the explosions of hefty pike smashing into the fry shoals rocked the surface mere feet away, suddenly sending my level of enthusiasm up several notches.

Peering down into the crystal clear water right alongside the staging, several good pike could be clearly seen slowly moving along the bottom, peering up menacingly at the fry shoals which were packed tightly together quite close to the surface of the water. Obviously a feeding spree was about to take place, so I lowered a smelt deadbait down to the bottom and jerked it enticingly upwards a couple of feet to see how the pike reacted. There then followed one of the most

There is nothing like being thrown in at the deep end for coming to grips with a situation quickly. Despite a late arrival at the lake, Tania soon found herself enjoying an apprenticeship with hard fighting pike which repeatedly tail-walked in and out of the reeds.

fascinating sessions I have ever had the privilege of witnessing. At such close range we could see every spot on the body of each pike and every move they made towards our twitched smelts. They bumped them gently with their noses, and even stood on their heads like tench, following the bait down to the bottom or actually grabbing hold on the drop. Initially their reactions were not those one expects from large predatory fish, although as the day progressed, all pike within the area became noticeably more aggressive. But that's how it seemed once we started to keep the hooks in. Takes were so incredibly tentative that the first three to suck in the twitched smelt all threw the hooks within seconds. Not that it mattered, because I believe we could have stood there hooking, losing and catching pike all day.

Tania's first fish (and her first ever pike) tipped the scales at around 12 lb, the second was slightly smaller. Her third was probably a little larger than the first, and soon after that we became so engrossed that we lost count, such was the euphoria. And they were all coming to twitched smelts. As I was about to slip the hooks from one of about 10 lb with forceps whilst it was still in the water, suddenly from right beneath the stagings came an incredibly long pike with an enormous head and shoulders, obviously intent on chomping the ten pounder. Fortunately, when only a few feet away, it saw us both directly overhead and returned from whence it came. In record time yet another smelt (we were running out fast) was mounted on the duo of size 8 barbless trebles and lowered down beside the rotting woodwork where we last saw the monster. A twitch was given, a slow pull, and then another twitch sending the smelt gyrating upwards, and as it spiralled tantalisingly from the bottom, like a flash the monster was upon it, flaring its huge gill plates as it sucked in the bait. Tania banged the hooks home perhaps with rather more force that I would have used on 11 lb test, and it shot off, fortunately out into the lake (I was concerned it would head straight between the staging supports) where it ripped line off the spool in three heavy surges making the clutch squeal. Now new to pike fishing she may well be, but after enjoying a quick apprenticeship with several acrobatic doubles already, Tania was not about to lose this one, and played it far more expertly than I have seen seasoned fishermen deal with big pike. Fortunately the hooks held throughout the long fight, with me issuing orders like a sergeant major (it's a fault of mine when behind the camera) to capture the best angles, and then it was all over. The incredibly long fish, 44" to be exact, was safely inside the big net. It looked well in excess of 25 lb, yet despite its massive head and shoulders, the body tapered away in rather a wasted appearance, cheating Tania of her first 20 pounder by a mere six ounces. Not that she was at all bothered about its weight; seeing such an impressive creature was reward enough, let alone actually catching it.

As the smelts started to run out with further pike, mostly all doubles, I rigged up a large copper spoon, whacked it out 50 yards and allowed it to touch bottom before starting the retrieve and handing the nine foot spinning rod over to Tania. Nothing happened until 10 yards from the staging when yet another pike grabbed hold – a nice one of close on 15½ lb. It seemed that in whatever direction the line was cast, pike were

Talk about beginner's luck. On her first ever serious pike fishing trip Tania lands a huge fish on twitched smelt dead bait. Measuring 44" there is no doubt that such a specimen must at some time have weighed considerably more than a shade under 20 lb.

there, lurking close by, rather like the red indians in a cowboy movie surrounding a wagon train.

I would have loved to stay and see if a really big fish put in an appearance; it was certainly the kind of day when it could happen, but we had promised to be back at the house for lunch by 2 pm, and so reluctantly we started to pack up. The last rod to be wound in was presenting a ledgered smelt which had been lying static on the bottom for at least two hours some 60 yards out, while all the commotion was going on at our feet. And would you believe it, just as I was about to lift it out, up popped a lovely fish of around 16 lb and promptly sucked it in. What a truly remarkable session; probably over 25 hits on both lures and twitched smelts, several lost pike and somewhere between 12 and 14 fish landed weighing into double figures. And all in little more than three hours of fun; I shall insist on taking Tania pike fishing again.

Tuesday 9

Mild, overcast and windy

Martin Founds and I met up amid the hustle and bustle of Heathrow's Terminal One at 11 am and were in Shannon Airport just two hours later. I never need much of an excuse to hop on a plane to the Emerald Isle, and I particularly love the Shannon region, with its superb all-round fishing.

Although we only had time for a short stay, our plan was an afternoon and morning's fishing in the company of Radio One D. J. Bruno Brookes, on his newly acquired lake set in beautiful woodlands half an hour's drive from the airport. Having fished with Bruno in New Zealand on a trout fishing research trip, Martin suggested that together we might be able to assist with an assessment of the pike fishing potential in the deep, mysterious-looking lake which had been left virtually unfished for over 30 years. In the course of a few impromptu sessions, Bruno had taken several fish just into double figures, and there was a tale of a local fisherman boasting a 32 pounder many years back. The lake certainly had pedigree and was indeed very deep, varying between ten and twenty feet down the middle throughout its entire length, with heavy beds of dwarf pond lily fringing the margins, over

Although Martin Founds, myself and our host, DJ Bruno Brookes, all failed to catch pike because of incessant rain and heavily coloured water, simply being afloat on such a beautifully matured Irish lake was reward enough.

which presided a wonderful array of old trees – oak, ash, chestnut, willow and sycamore.

Prospects, apart from the weather, seemed promising. But deep, peaty-looking water with only minimal visibility (about six inches) and very low-lying clouds soaking us from the moment we shoved the boat off in that horrible fine rain, meant our chances of getting stuck into anything worthwhile were probably rather slim. And so it proved.

In the afternoon we wobbled deadbaits (I had taken along some smelts in a freezer bag) close to the bottom in the deep channel, popped surface lures both in and beside the fringe of marginal lilies, trolled up and down with big spoons and deep diving plugs, all without so much as a tap.

Unfortunately, the following morning saw almost a repeat performance. Bruno had to rush off early to catch a plane to London for a *Top of The Pops* show, leaving the entire lake to Martin and myself. Instead of clearing as we had hoped, the rain became unbearably heavy after an hour or so, and apart from one half-hearted hit by a tiny pike to a large surface popper twitched through the lilies up at the shallow end, that was it. We shall have to wait for another time to see what the lake can produce.

VIVA ESPAÑA

In recent weeks and for perhaps as far back as the last three months, my fishing has been rather disjointed to say the least. Since starting a new television series with the Canadian trip back at the end of July, I have found organising local sessions on a regular basis almost impossible. There has been so much to do behind the scenes to ensure that the *Go Fishing* programmes work smoothly that I really haven't had the time for any serious trips after pike and zander which under normal circumstances would be receiving my attention now that autumn has arrived. But then again, I love the diversity and the challenge of trying to catch fish to order from different parts of the world, and so rising this morning at 5 am to make the long drive down to Heathrow

15 Monday

airport stimulated more enthusiasm than rising early to fish the Norfolk Broads. Our destination this time was Spain.

The two hour flight to Barcelona with Iberian Airlines went smoothly and surprisingly quickly and we were soon installed in our hire cars. Although the road signs were rather confusing for a few miles after leaving the airport, giving us the option of taking at least five different roads to reach the same place (and only one was the fast route), we soon found our way onto the A7 heading due south through Tarragona and towards our final destination, San Carlos near the town of Amposta. After a two and a half hour drive on fast, excellent motorways, we were met at the Carlos III hotel by friends Terry Smith and Martin Founds of *Anglers World Holidays*, who had arrived two days earlier for the sole purpose of reconnoitring the current fishing prospects.

By the expression on Martin's usually jovial face when I enquired eagerly about the fishing, sport had obviously been slow. The River Ebro, which is up to 200 yards wide and

Below: When filming Go Fishing *I am always surrounded by technicians and video equipment, but somehow I manage to produce the goods regardless.*

Below right: The River Ebro is stuffed full of fish: carp to over 30 lb, chub, barbel, large-mouth bass, catfish and enormous shoals of sizeable grey mullet, like this fly-caught specimen.

Facing page: Viva España! It may look as though I took this fine common carp from a secluded rocky pool . . . but not so.

146

varies from 10 to over 40 feet deep, is jam-packed full of wild carp ranging from 2 to over 20 lbs and barbel in the 1–6 lbs range, plus hordes of mullet and a few chub. It was currently running very low and on the clear side, and the fish were simply not responding as they should have been. Terry and Martin had only been able to interest the occasional barbel and carp. So we all trudged along to the bar before dinner to work out a realistic plan of action to make the best of difficult circumstances.

Tuesday 16

Very hot and sunny. Gentle breeze.

We all rose early and after a typical Spanish breakfast of croissants, fruit juice and black coffee, drove up through the mountains following the path of the Ebro to Xerta to shoot some quiver tipping sequences. This was a fabulous location where the river runs exceptionally deep through a picturesque wooded valley lined with groves of pomegranites, olives, tangerines and oranges. Only ten yards out from the rocky outcrop where I sat, the water was over 30 feet deep with a good 15 feet immediately beneath the rod tip.

Sport, as Terry and Martin had predicted, was nowhere near as fast and furious as I would have liked, but a small barbel, followed by a couple of carp to around 5 lbs on quiver tipped corn gave the cameras some nice action material – all in technicolour sunshine. The Ebro valley is a majestic location, with massive beds of ten foot high Spanish reeds lining the steep banks, overhanging willows and numerous flowering shrubs. From above Xerta, water is taken and fed along both sides of the valley through concrete-banked irrigation channels all the way down to the Delta Ebre, a huge wetland between Amposta and the Mediterranean. This nature reserve, rich in flora and fauna, is the second largest in Europe, next to the Algarve.

After lunch we crossed the river at Tortosa and followed the Ebro's course upstream along the north bank to the huge dam and weir at Tiveneys, to run off some scenic shots and the tackle log. In previous series of *Go Fishing*, criticism has been made of the fact that we have never shown the tackle I use in enough detail, so we are trying to put this right.

Then it was a long slog back to the hotel for dinner, with at least a portion of the programme in the can. However both Martin and I were worried that the river was decidedly out of sorts; the carp and barbel were certainly not moving as expected. So for tomorrow we are to use the 'banker' swim at the 'gusher', right in the middle of Amposta. Here one of the irrigation channels spews its water back into the Ebro, a little way upstream from the main road bridge by the old town wall, attracting massive concentrations of barbel, carp, mullet and the occasional American black bass.

17 Wednesday

Sunny and very hot all day.

Terry Smith and I rose long before the others to be at the gusher for the crack of dawn. We wanted to see if we could put the carp and barbel into a feeding mood with some heavy baiting of cereal balls laced with corn and barley. Fish were characteristically rolling everywhere and prospects for filming looked extremely promising, but we could not buy a bite at any price. Carp and some sizeable fish were coming up to the surface and simply laughing at us. Where the gusher entered the river just to our right the surface was crammed with thousands of large mullet. Talk about fish soup; it was difficult to believe our plight.

When the crew arrived and Paul asked how many we had caught there was not a lot we could say. The situation was almost laughable, except that I did not feel much like laughing. Here was a river full of fish where on previous occasions Terry and I had bagged massive hauls of carp into double figures and barbel over 6 lb. We talked about the possibility of reduced oxygen levels since the river was so low, and whether the compensation water being introduced further upstream could have affected the fish responding, but did not come up with any answers.

When the cameras were set up we decided to start filming some scene shots in the hope that the situation would change. After a few minutes I happened to notice a carp come skidding down the steep concrete weir behind me, obviously from the irrigation channel above which was getting lower and lower; it plunged into a small rocky pool foaming with white water. Could there be carp in this shallow pool full of rocks – the most unlikely looking carp swim anyone could imagine? Were they more inclined to feed here in the clearer water than in the main river itself, into which water from the pool flowed mere yards away? There was only one way to find out, and so the camera positions were rearranged to cover the pool while I crouched amongst the rocks and lowered a piece of breakflake on a size 6 hook tied direct to 6 lb test into the foaming white water. Two AA shots pinched on the line 10 inches above the hook were just enough to hold amongst the rocks and keep the bait static. But not for long. All at once the line held in my left hand twitched as the rod tip was yanked over hard. With less than 10 feet of line out from rod tip to bait, I responded with a gentle strike and we were in business as a common carp of about 2 lb shot around the pool.

I am sure everyone thought this was simply fluke, but five more common carp (there are very few mirrors and leathers in the Ebro) up to 8 lb followed, and some exciting fights turned what seemed a hopeless situation into an extremely interesting section of the programme. Above all it proved the crucial importance of opportunism in fishing. No piece of water, no matter how small or insignificant, should ever be overlooked.

After lunch we visited the harbour in San Carlos, which boasts the second largest fishing fleet in the whole of the Mediterranean, to film a short local interest spot for the programme. When I first researched the Ebro Valley, the fish market with its hustle and bustle, bartering and unbelievable array of colourful sea fishes really held my attention. Finally being able to make it part of my presentation for *Go Fishing* was something I had been looking forward to.

Thursday 18

Very hot with bright sunshine all day.

It has indeed been 'sunny Spain' throughout our filming. Whilst rain can often be heard against the window panes during the night, when we rise in the morning the skies have cleared and the sun beats down bright and incredibly hot for the entire day. With today being the third and final day of the shoot, it was imperative that we drive back up into the mountains early to the weir at Tiveneys to film some mullet fishing on the fly rod.

Catching what is a sea fish (although it travels far inland) on the fly rod in such breathtaking scenery would add a wonderful section to our programme, particularly as the weather was so glorious. With the river so low there were simply dozens of tempting little pools and fast bubbly runs immediately beneath the main sill, which was all of 300 yards long; I could easily have spent the entire day there working from one shoal of mullet to another. There were thousands of fish, all in the one to four pounds bracket, plus a sprinkling of American large mouth bass. Having been stocked into Spanish waters some years back these bass have spread throughout the Ebro system adding an interesting bonus fish, especially for spinning and fly rodding enthusiasts. The two which sucked in a wet size 12 coachman which worked so effectively with the mullet, were only a few ounces apiece, though I have been informed these bass are taken to 5 lb plus from the Ebro, and twice the size from a few lakes in the mountains. Their presence certainly seems worth some exploration in the future.

After catching several nice mullet, which scrapped extremely hard in the foaming white water (though their takes on the wet fly were gentler than I had expected), we had more than enough in the can. At lunchtime we stopped, making our way to the ancient city of Tortosa and to the Parador, where the outros and final part of the programme were to be filmed from the castle walls high above the old city which afford a breathtaking view over the Ebro Valley.

Due to fatigue and the fact that I am not used to remembering lines (the programme relies on my being able to ad lib continually), we needed to shoot several takes before I finally managed to remember what I had written, and reel off to camera the facts about how to get the most from the Catalunya region. I have yet to use idiot (prompting) boards, and though I think this would make things very much easier, the way we shoot the outros comes off more naturally, even if it takes a little longer.

And so apart from the long drive back to Barcelona the following morning, yet another *Go Fishing* was completely in the can. I really enjoyed our Spanish shoot and look forward to seeing the demo tape once Paul has put it together.

Very warm, bright sunshine.

The unbelievably deep, blue waters off Madeira attract huge concentrations of skipjack, big-eyed and blue fin tuna, not to mention marlin at certain times of the year. This colourful array of artificial trolling lures can be used to tempt them.

One of the nice things about making programmes for television is that simultaneously I need to be thinking and working at least a year in advance, researching others. Tania and I were therefore only too pleased to exchange four cold and blustery days in Britain for the warmth, flowers, wine, scenery and excellent food of Madeira.

I had been meaning to visit my old pal Roddy Hayes of Alderney for some time. Roddy helped make one of the programmes in series two of *Go Fishing* when we wreck-fished for big cod and ling in the deep waters off the Channel Islands. But in the meantime, Roddy has up and moved to Porto Santo, an island just 25 miles north east of Madeira, where he now runs a big game fishing boat. So we decided to mix business and pleasure. Our plan on reaching Funchal, the capital of Madeira, was to take the ferry over to Porto Santo, enjoy a couple of days on Roddy's boat and then return for a day's sightseeing back in Madeira to sort out some pretty intros for any proposed programme that might evolve as a result of our visit. It all worked out very neatly.

Unfortunately, the fishing was not exceptional, but then I had already been warned that only small skipjack tuna were really on the cards, with an outside chance of a yellow fin if we went offshore trolling. This is exactly what happened. At least Tania enjoyed her first taste of blue water game fishing and was amazed at just how fast and powerful even a baby tuna of 6 or 7 lb can be, compared to freshwater fish of identical size.

Roddy suggested that the best time for making a programme would be during April or May when the unbelievably clear, deep, blue waters around these islands (formed by volcanic eruptions) enjoy good numbers of both blue fin and big-eyed tuna, plus the occasional marlin; Roddy's boat *Anguilla* had accounted for blue marlin to over 500 lb during the summer. I decided the best bet for our programmes would be to take advantage of the prolific run of big-eyes. Ranging from 30 lb to over 100 lb they would put up a long, hard and exciting fight for the cameras.

Roddy also suggested we visit the local fish market back in Funchal to see what else was on show from the local waters. Obviously we should have arrived when the market was really humming at 6 am when all the catches of big fish are on show. Nevertheless, even at 11 am we still enjoyed having a look round at the sharks, tuna, sardines and various oddities, including the weirdest black scabbard fish, a regional delicacy served up in all the local restaurants. I am sure, however, that most diners would never lift up their knives and forks were they to see the scabbard fish prior to filleting. It averages between four and five feet long with a jet black, smooth eel-like body and an enormous head full of long barracuda-type teeth. Its huge eyes are proof that the scabbard hunts in very deep water. I can remember catching a rather similar creature called a hairtail from the tidal reaches of the Hawkesbury River near Sydney many years ago, except that hairtails were the normal eel-grey colour. But they too lived in very deep water and were equally prehistoric in appearance.

All in all, this was a most rewarding research trip, and I look forward to visiting Roddy in the not-too-distant future to do battle with the larger tuna. Landing back in Britain after four days in the hot sun always promotes a negative feeling, which makes me wish I lived in the tropics again. But I shouldn't really complain – next Friday our crew is off to The Gambia to make yet more programmes.

My old pal, Roddy Hayes, who runs charter trips from Porto Santo was right: only skipjack tuna were really on the cards during the short research trip. Tania boated a lively six pounder.

THE GAMBIA REVISITED

Friday 2

The euphoria of catching a plane to fish in distant countries will always be there for me; but it is greatly diminished when the check-in time is at the unearthly hour of 5 am.

The only change in crew on this trip is second cameraman Peter Milic with whom I have not worked before. The others, Paul, Dave, Jamie and Melissa were all waiting at the desk in the south terminal the following morning, faces beaming as usual, ready to depart with Britannia Airlines.

At last the time to revisit the wonderful saltwater fishing of The Gambia had arrived. You will recall that way back at the beginning of January (it seems such a long time ago now), Martin Founds and I researched the waters of the mighty Gambia River system with future television programmes in mind. Now it was proof of the pudding time; with ten days ahead (including flights) our intention is to shoot enough material for two separate programmes, showing the enormous diversity of inshore and offshore fishing in The Gambia, plus a smattering of local interest. Pressure of time had prevented Martin and I from getting amongst the sharks and rays back in January; this is something I hope to experience on this trip along with fun from the barracuda and snappers of the mangrove swamps, not to mention some hefty offshore species on the medium boat outfits. It's a great pity that Martin, who organised both trips, found commitments with his travel business too pressing to slip away on this occasion. His professional handling of hotel and airline problems is always a great advantage when travelling.

Saturday 3

Baking hot all day.

We breakfasted early by the pool and after a short drive to Denton Bridge where *White Warrior*, skippered by Mark Longster is moored, attempted the introductory shots of yours truly, laden with tackle, walking just 20 yards from the bus to the beach where a group of local youngsters were ready with a large canoe to ferry me out to the fishing boat. I say attempted, because every time we were

An aquarium fish whole-saler could make a fortune in the Gambia River system. Fishing the mangroves with fish strip produced an exotic oddity on almost every cast during the filming of the Go Fishing *programmes.*

set up and ready to go, a busload of tourists would come into frame and all hell broke loose. It was certainly not the kind of fracas we wanted on the first day, but eventually, taking two hours to accomplish what should have taken just 20 minutes, we were finally on our way for a shark fishing sortie. Mark's boat had taken sharks on almost every day recently, using a special rubby dubby method when lying at anchor some 4 miles out in the mouth of the river in 60 feet of water. Everyday except today that is. For at least five hours, almost the duration of the entire ebbing tide, we expected the baits to go at any second, but it was not to be. Still, we all gained nice suntans and I took a couple of small reef fishes messing about with the lighter rod.

Mark's rubby dubby, which consists of dozens of chopped up bonga fish mixed in with cod liver oil, is not simply tossed over the side of the boat with a ladle to set up a surface oil slick – the accepted method of shark attraction. The tide flow in the Gambia River is so strong that the attractor would soon be lost and taken miles away, with next to no chance of sharks following the slick up to the boat and over the ledgered baits – whole bongas on a size 10/0 with a flapping fillet either side.

Above: Barracuda are equipped with the kind of dentistry that could remove your fingers in seconds. Look at the scars on this diving plug.

Above right: Why nature has given the strange looking Kujeli (captain fish) a transparent nose is a complete mystery.

Right: Who's a silly boy then? . . . With a rusty size 3/0 treble firmly embedded past the barb in his fore-finger, Wilson had to stop trolling and head for the hospital.

Facing page: Though far from being representative of the species in terms of size, this 15 lb barracuda, caught trolling with diving plugs, provided excellent material for the TV cameras.

The simple method for getting the mix down is to rig up a spare rod with a heavy lead and to pass the lead through a hole made in the bottom of a large polythene carrier bag. The bag is then secured tight around the lead and filled with rubby dubby. When lowered over the side and down to the bottom, water pressure alone folds down the open top around the rubby dubby which then does not spill out as might be expected. When the lead and bag touch the bottom, a couple of heavy jerks invert the bag and all the contents spill out, creating a wonderful attractor line right there on the bottom where the baits are. Naturally, as most of the pieces drift downtide while others become lodged between the rocks, the sharks follow this smelly food line right up to the baits. Today they obviously were not hungry.

Sunday 4

Baking hot all day.

As the start of the ebb was not until 1 pm and there was little point in getting out in the river mouth to try for the sharks until then, we decided to start the beginning of what will be the first programme by dinghy fishing the mangrove channels. That's the beauty of the huge potential within the Gambia River system. There is such a diversity — from inexpensive dinghy fishing with cut bait for snappers and the like, to full-blooded big game fishing on sport fishing boats such as Mark's. There is something to suit everyone.

As always time simply flew by and as we needed to leave the mangroves for the hour long trip to the sharking grounds by noon, I had but half an hour of snapper fishing before having to pull anchor. The intro shots of the mangroves had taken (as usual) much longer than expected, but we did have some very nice footage in the can. Shooting in sunshine really does make everything look so beautiful and coming to the tropics to film with guaranteed weather, compared to sea fishing off the east coast of Britain for example, immediately cuts continuity problems by half. We can shoot the fishing one day and then, knowing the weather will be the same, return on the following day for all the pick up shots. Since this shoot is just a one camera shoot we have no alternative. Long-winded and frustrating it may be but it produces the goods.

By 2 pm the tide was really starting to ebb fast and with *White Warrior* firmly anchored right in the mouth of the river in 60 feet of water, Mark put down several bags full of rubby dubby. We then put three baits over on 2 lb leads to keep them on the bottom and sat back to await events. Fortunately action was not long in coming and the first shark run fair sizzled line from Mark's 50 lb class wide Shimano lever drag reel. I had to wait several seconds before hitting the run on camera, while Dave Lindsay turned the transmitter on in my shirt pocket which works the radio microphone hidden in the shirt's button hem. Unfortunately the shark had taken too much line when I finally attempted to bang the hook home. There is an incredible amount of stretch in 100 yards of line and the shark was fully this distance away when I struck. It was on for perhaps 30 seconds and then the line fell slack. However Mark assured us that where there was one, more would be following the scent trail uptide. How right he was. Suddenly the Penn 9/0 holding 75 lb line on my heavy rod screeched into action and I was on it like a flash, banging the hook home before the camera was even ready to shoot. But more problems; this shark, which felt extremely big, was certainly well-hooked but it managed to thread the trace around some rocks and then around my other line. It was on for slightly longer than the first before the line fell limp again. By now everyone was well and truly gutted and starting to believe that the odds were stacked against us. Upon reeling in the 250 lb cable laid wire trace we saw that it had been severed completely about four inches above the hook. Not to be outdone, out went the three baits again (the other two are wound in as soon as a shark is hooked) and Mark put down another two bags of rubby dubby. Time was marching on. Then, quite suddenly, with that startling noise made only by big fish tearing off, the reel on my big rod started to shriek. This time my strike was quick and brutally hard, heaving the fish up and away from those rocks as fast as I could manage. The power of whatever was on the other end felt awesome, and seeing it was a big fish Mark quickly buoyed the anchor so that we could drift with the shark – otherwise I would be fighting both shark and a four to five knot tide. As far as the filming was concerned it was mayhem; with the boat rocking violently in the fresh breeze, even standing up straight was difficult and as the run was so quick there was no time to film the line screaming from the reel and me winding down to the shark to strike. Within a few minutes we were a quarter of a mile away from the buoyed anchor and drifting fast, the shark as powerful as when it was first hooked. At least I was able to keep it away from the bottom and the sanctuary of the jagged rocks whenever it got its head down and dived; but my aching arms paid heavily. In fact after three quarters of an hour the thought crossed my mind, as indeed it does all anglers at some time during a hard saltwater battle, that it might have been better had I never hooked this brute.

Against Mark's advice I was not using the fighting chair and harness or even a butt pad. The shark had taken the bait offered (as I hoped it would) on my old 7 foot big game rod and Penn 9/0 Senator loaded with 75 lb test. This was an outfit I first used, dare I say it, over 25 years ago when serving a spell in the Merchant Navy, and later when living on the island of Barbados. The rod, which I actually made from a big game Marlin tip, had served me well and was specifically constructed for playing big fish from the beach and from high up on the side of our cruise ship the *SS Oronsay*. By sticking the long butt between my legs, thus lowering the position of the reel, there is no chance of toppling forward and two hands can be used on the grip above the reel for heaving. On the beach it works particularly well for walking down towards the fish whilst gaining line, and then walking backwards for long heavy pumps. However within the limited deck of Mark's 28 footer I was having to strain with my arms and back far more. At one stage Mark even offered to give me a breather, but didn't ask again once he'd seen the look on my face. I am not, I like to think, an aggressive person by nature, but link me up to a creature which is fighting hard and I know I change. There is no way I would ever hand the rod over to anyone.

After 55 minutes and a drift of almost two miles I finally managed to pump the unseen shark up for Mark to grab the 12 foot leader. The 2 lb lead was quickly detached and the leader raised slowly hand over hand. With the Gambia River being so coloured through a constant stream of sediment flowing down from far upriver, visibility is less than two feet. This meant that the shark's size was not revealed until its massive head with flared gill slits finally broke surface in a mountain of spray. Mark was nearly pulled overboard as the shark, a big lemon of 280–300 lb crashed its eight foot frame against *White Warrior*, then he could hold the trace no longer and the great fish sounded once more.

The film crew, who until this moment had really no idea what a big shark looks like at close range, were ecstatic. There were hoots and cheers which I secretly hoped were not premature for I had yet to bring the beast up again. Seeing the boat had given it a new lease of life, something I could have done with at that particular moment.

After another ten minutes the shark was ready for the surface again and this time Mark managed to hold on while we shot close ups of its enormous jaws as it thrashed the surface to foam. Now came the tricky part. I had no intention of going through the usual motions of using the flying gaff and roping the shark up for return to harbour. It was my intention to show the television viewer that sharks did not have to be killed (although it's not easy explaining this to a hungry African who simply wishes to eat), and so Mark leaned perilously over the gunnel, gripping the hook with a pair of pliers and actually unhooked it in the water. We had expected to cut the wire but the hook was in fact just outside the jaws, making a clean unhooking possible. Slowly the great lemon shark sunk beneath the waves and Paul said 'cut'. We had it all in the bag and everyone went crazy. Handshakes and congratulations all round after what was certainly the most exciting filming session to date.

A fter yesterday's jackpot we had earned a late start and so after an 8 am breakfast by the pool Paul, Melissa and myself watched the rushes to see what we did have in the can and which fill-in shots were still required. Fortunately there were not many, but a return to the sharking grounds was necessary and so we set off from Denton Bridge aboard *White Warrior* with a large tub of bonga fish bait to catch the start of the ebb at around 1 pm.

At a little after 1 pm we lowered the anchor amongst the rocks in the deep water shark mark and chopped up a huge

5 Monday

Baking hot all day.

bucketful of bongas for rubby dubby to use once the tide was ebbing strongly. For an hour or so we systematically shot all the cut-ins to match with what went on yesterday – tackle presentation etc (it's a one camera shoot remember), and then put the baits out on the same three rods as used yesterday with the intention of taking a few linking fillers to match with what was already in the can. But before Paul and Peter could move the camera and switch boats to one of Mark's much smaller trolling crafts, one of the rods started to screech as a shark belted downtide with the bait. As luck would have it it was on my long rod, the very same outfit on which I caught the shark yesterday. The situation could not have been better if we had planned it, though still feeling the aftermath of yesterday's battle with every muscle in my arms screaming out, I did not exactly relish a repeat performance. That however is exactly what I got.

Since our programme could not possibly prove creditable with the capture of two huge sharks appearing in just one episode of 26 minutes, this was a wonderful opportunity for some mixing and matching. I was stuck into a similar sized shark, hooked on the same gear and in the same spot; even sea and weather conditions were identical. Halfway through the fight Mark whispered in my ear: 'there's no way this one's going back John'. Apparently yesterday evening he had to sit all his local crew down and explain why we had to unhook the shark and let it go because all they could see was good food being wasted. If we did the same again we were likely to have a mutiny on board; after all, Gambians who sea fish for a living eat all that's caught and see no reason why shark meat should not be eaten along with everything else. Of course their point is valid and so we had little reason for returning without the shark, another 'lemon'. When it came alongside after almost an hour's fight, I thought at first that it was larger than yesterday's. The beast was incredibly thick across the shoulders and required three of us to haul it over the gunnel once the flying gaff was in. Yet upon our return to the moorings when we hoisted it up on the scales it made 220 lb. That however still makes up a very large fish.

With the largest part of programme two now finished, I fancied some general offshore boat fishing to front the excitement of shark fishing and so we boarded *White Warrior* once again and dropped anchor just off the shipping lane in 50 feet of water where the ground is particularly rocky. Mark and I were fishing five different outfits from 15 lb test to 50 lb, each either fillets of fresh bongas or small whole mullet. I took two fish in fairly quick succession and these were followed by a long lull. However we could not have hoped for a more interesting pair. The first was a catfish of around 3 lb and the second a captain fish which has the local name of kujeli. This unusual fish has a transparent, pointed nose above an underslung toothless mouth, and huge fins. This one weighed around 6–7 lb but they are regularly taken between 20 and 40 lb. Mark's boat has in fact accounted for a real monster kujeli which pulled the scales down to 120 lb; what a brute that must have been and what a fight.

The reader might recall that when researching the Gambia River back in January, I took a brace of beautifully coloured casarva fish. I had rather hoped one would put in an appearance on camera but it was not to be. I did however connect momentarily with something exceptionally meaty on a 15 lb outfit but the hook came out when it had travelled just a few yards. What would really have made the day if Mark had managed to hang on, was a huge fish which picked up a whole bonga on a 10/0 hook and 150 lb wire trace (intended for sting ray) and with tremendous speed and power steamed off uptide ripping over 100 yards of line from Mark's reel. It was too fast for a ray and too erratic for a shark. Mark was yelling out that it would be a giant snapper or maybe even a monster kujeli when suddenly the line fell back slack. We thought the trace must have been severed on the rocks into which this particular monster was continually diving, hence our guess that it was a huge snapper, yet the hook was still there. Nonetheless it was all wonderful action for the camera. Of course fishing is about catching big fish, but as we all know it is about losing them as well and I think it is nice to show the heartaches as well as the joy. Mark really was sick about losing that fish and he went on about the fact all the way back to the moorings.

6 Tuesday

Baking hot all day.

Wednesday 7

Baking hot all day, fresh wind.

Things are so relaxed out here in the Gambia that it's easy to forget the fact that I am supposed to be working. Thus whilst I would have chosen to return offshore to the deep water mark where Mark pulled out of that unseen monster yesterday, there were some pick-up shots to be done in the mangroves to complete the first half of programme one.

By ten o' clock I had anchored the dinghy in exactly the same spot as on Sunday and with the last three hours of the incoming tide ahead we were hopeful of catching some interesting fish. I was secretly hoping that a colourful red snapper would turn up on the strips of mullet ledgered slightly down tide, or maybe even a barracuda. But I simply could not get the bait past casarva to about 2 lb, small kujeli, sunpat fish and a strange, extremely thin, but very deep fish which if you were into saltwater aquariums would cost an arm and a leg to purchase in the UK. It was however all nice, relaxed filming until someone on the camera boat snapped one of my light rods off six inches above the butt cap. It could of course have been repaired had it not followed whatever was on the other end overboard, complete with reel. Trying to look relaxed and happy in front of the camera is of course part of my job as presenter of *Go Fishing* but believe me it takes some doing when underneath the calm expression you are seething with rage.

We finished all the mangrove creek fill-ins by around 3 pm which allowed plenty of time to motor across the habour, to film what remains of *Radio Caroline*. I doubt if any of its former crew and DJs would ever be able to recognise the collapsed, rusted hulk now, but it was nice anyway to get things right.

Thursday 8

Baking hot all day.

If there is one thing that is certain about the Gambia it is the consistency of the weather. Every single day starts with clear skies and a gentle breeze and then by around eleven in the morning the breeze dies away, leaving the sun to beat down for the entire day. It was lovely therefore to be out trolling all day in search of barracuda, casarvas and red snapper. However it was disappointing that after six hours of trolling both offshore beyond Denton Bridge and through miles of mangroves, that all we had to show for our efforts at the end of the afternoon was one 10 lb barracuda. I did bang into two large red snappers, only to have both come off mere feet away from the boat. It was a bitter disappointment because had we managed to film both of these we would by now have most of the first programme in the can.

A s the sea had flattened right off we made an instant decision at the moorings to spend an hour or so working the pool just outside Denton Bridge and then drive south over the sand bars to troll up and down the coastline in search of barracuda and jacks.

We tried big spoons, jet heads and a variety of diving plugs with four rods continually out, yet by lunchtime not a strike had come our way. We carried on in a southerly direction and eventually came upon a series of sand bars about half a mile offshore with deep channels between. Here we struck gold. Simultaneously two of the rods arched over as the reels screamed out and within seconds, from absolutely nothing, Mark and I were both into good fish. Unfortunately Mark's came off within 50 yards of the boat so we concentrated upon mine for the camera. I was hoping for a large jack crevalle and by the way the fish was keeping deep and shaking its head I was sure my wish had been answered. But as it came up from beneath the stern with the large blue rapala firmly embedded in its awesome jaws, we could see that it was indeed a fine 5 lb barracuda.

On the next hit, again to my rod, we certainly got action but not of the kind I had anticipated. There is always danger from flying hooks on the large, deep diving plugs as a barracuda is hauled on board, they are such a lively fish. Their dentistry alone is enough to command instant respect; one slip with a finger or thumb and those razor teeth will amputate as cleanly as a surgeon's scalpel. I am therefore usually extremely careful when handling and unhooking this fine fighter. As my fish came alongside we saw that it was in

9 Friday

Baking hot all day. Flat calm out at sea.

There comes a time in each and every fight with a big shark when you start to wish you had never hooked it. After 30 minutes of blood, sweat and tears whilst gaining and losing line, I had almost reached that point.

fact a foul-hooked barracuda which Mark immediately hauled overboard and deposited in the bottom of the boat. One of the trebles was embedded in the rear of its head and so holding its shoulders tight to the boards with my left hand I endeavoured to work the treble out with a pair of pliers held in my right hand. Then in a split second, it happened. Paul said he heard my scream from the camera boat over 100 yards away. I had committed the cardinal error of stupidity and not let go of the pliers when the lively barracuda squirmed and flapped beneath my left hand, instantly pulling the other size 3/0 treble of the rapala deep diver into my right index finger. It was embedded a good way past the barb. I was now

A fresh bonga fish mounted on a size 10/0 hook with a fillet on each side makes a fine shark bait.

At last, after an hour of playing the big lemon shark standing up without a harness or butt pad (serves me right), I relax whilst skipper Mark Longster grabs the trace.

connected to the diving plug, the other end of which was still connected to a flapping barracuda of around 10 lb. Mark instantly saw my plight and while I closed my left hand in a dead man's grip to hold the fish still, he used my strong wire cutters (purchased for the purpose of cutting the wire close to the hook in the shark trace if necessary) to snip through the eye of the hook and detach it from the split ring. Two snips and I sat back to survey the situation, which I already knew was far from good. The huge rusty treble created a problem beyond anything we might attempt to treat with first aid and so Paul immediately made the decision to wrap filming and get me straight to a hospital. Fortunately we had just about enough in the can for the trolling section of programme one (thank goodness), although another two hours trolling might well have produced one of the large jacks I was hoping to get stuck into. I did offer to snip the hook off at the bend and continue but Paul would have none of it and so we beached the boat and caught a taxi to the nearest hospital.

After finding the hospital's reception we waited in line behind all the locals before one kind gentleman saw the hook protruding from my finger and beckoned us to the head of the queue. The woman before us, so the reception clerk stated, was a self-confessed lunatic and once she had been led away we were given a slip of paper to see a particular surgeon. I was told to lie relaxed on the operating trolley while the young doctor prepared a local anaesthetic for my finger with the special sterilised needle and swab pack we always carry when travelling outside Europe. All seemed well until the young doctor stuck the needle into my already extremely painful finger. It was worse than the hook going in and the hypodermic syringe fell apart as he was pressing the plunger. All this I could see from the corner of one eye whilst lying down, so I quickly sat up and pulled the needle out just as he was preparing to plunge in further, having put the syringe back together. Air had obviously entered the syringe and there was no way that Wilson was ready for an air embolism and that big floating river in the sky.

At this point tempers were about to flare, especially mine. I asked the doctor what he proposed to do once the anesthetic had frozen my finger. Naturally I assumed, having been through the rigmarole two years back when a treble connected to a jumping trout (in the very same finger by coincidence) was stuck fast past the barb, that he would push the point all the way through the nail and snip it off past the barb. The hook could then simply be eased out the way it had entered. But no, this guy was going to slit the entire ball of the finger right down to the wire and stitch it up again. I decided upon a bit of home surgery. I held the other two prongs of the hook with my left hand and, despite the look on Paul's face saying 'do you really want to do this?' forced the point and barb of the hook out through the top of the nail. It was now ready to be snipped off and I nodded towards the medical equipment tray (which held fewer tools than I carry in my tackle bag) and to a large pair of what looked like snips. The doctor had now cottoned on and enthusiastically pressed the snips together with the power of his two hands, but nothing happened. I just could not believe the situation. There I was, sitting on the edge of the trolley with the point and barb of a rusty 3/0 treble protruding from my forefinger with the local anaesthetic decidedly starting to wear off. Paul (bless him) said he would run back to the hotel to see if the others had returned with my fishing bag and powerful wire cutters.

For a good 15 minutes I just sat there pondering the ludicrous, almost (almost) laughable situation while every doctor on the floor came along to ponder the case. The door was then flung open and Paul rushed in carrying my fishing bag and powerful wire cutters, absolutely drenched in sweat but with the smile on his face saying 'I've done it'. And indeed he had. He offered my cutters to the doctor who this time severed the forged hook with a loud crack. Instantly I pulled the shank of the treble out the way it had entered and sat back with a sigh of relief. It was over. What a day!

With most of the two programmes now well in the can, today was used for shooting a number of pick-up shots that we badly needed for continuity. The first was to be a wide shot of me fishing back in the mangroves and so I anchored the dinghy in the same spot as a few days ago and enjoyed 15 minutes fishing while waiting for the camera boat to set up and come alongside. It was with no small touch

10 Saturday

Baking hot all day.

of irony therefore that I should actually bang into two fish, of a size I was incapable of hooking when we filmed the creek piece. The first came to the light outfit on ledgered fish strip, it was a nice sized casarva which was unfortunately savaged off the hook by a barracuda on the way in. Then the 20 lb outfit, presenting a large fillet of Bonga was away. It felt like a very large snapper by the dogged way it was fighting, but I never saw it. Suddenly the line fell slack; the fish had slipped the hook. And as far as the rest of my fishing went, that was that. For the remainder of the day we shot various intros and outros, visiting the famous crocodile pool to stroke and play with Henry the friendly croc and a fishing village along the south coast to see the local boats land their catches of sharks and rays. With only a short outro to shoot on Monday morning before we have to leave (I could stay here for very much longer), tomorrow has been designated a day off, so I am spending an entire day out bottom fishing offshore for sharks and anything else which happens along – without the cameras.

Sunday 11

Baking hot all day.

Mark and I got off to an early start, loading all our gear into one of the 19 foot Orkney fast liners (fabulous fishing boats for the tropics) and headed off under Denton Bridge to the sharking grounds in the middle of the Gambia River's mouth. By 10 am we had put down several loads of rubby dubby and had six baits out; four rods for shark and two light outfits. Within minutes I banged into a couple of kujeli on bonga fillet on the light outfit – the larger was around 6 lb – while Mark accounted for a couple of small catfish. Then one of Mark's shark baits was taken and he quickly struck into what looked to be a hefty fish, by the amount of line it took, for about 30 seconds before it managed to slip the hook. Shortly after this my lightest shark outfit was away and I banged the hook home on the first run. On 40 lb test this small shark, a lemon, put up a super scrap for a fish barely making 50 lb, but was inside the boat within 5 minutes.

By now the ebbing tide was about to turn and we started to bring the rods in for a move from the 60 foot deep gully to a 45 foot rocky plateau some 400 yards away. I was about to reel in the light (30 lb) outfit when the rod tip started to 'knock' from the typical way in which sting rays take the bait by smothering it first, then sucking it in. I struck as the line moved off and the heavy resistance came alive as the ray headed away from the boat. For about 5 minutes I was well in the game and enjoyed a lovely spot of cat and mouse; the ray was not massive – perhaps 30–40 lb – and on 30 lb test, nicely manageable. Then, quite suddenly, the hook came out. It was going to be one of those days.

After a change of anchorage and several more lost fish, out went all the rods again along with several helpings of rubby dubby. We had decided to call it a day at 5.30 pm and almost on the minute the rod tip on my 50 lb outfit started knocking. I sprang up, knocked the ratchet off and allowed the shark to rip off a good 30 feet before slamming the reel into gear and leaning back into it. I was disappointed, the fish came too easily towards me, higher and higher up through the water feeling very much like a small ray and just knocking the rod tip every now and then. But Mark had buoyed the anchor anyway and as we drifted towards the small ray it must suddenly have caught sight of the boat's shadow overhead. In a split second it came to life and miraculously changed into a very large shark indeed, ripping close on 200 yards of line from the reel in one long, surging run. It was heading uptide fast and so Mark started the engine to give chase. Wilson was going to do the business after all on the very last cast of the last day's fishing in the Gambia.

By now there was no doubt that the shark knew it was hooked. It doubled back to the boat time and time again before belting off against the tide in long and completely unstoppable runs, just when I thought my efforts were making an impression. After a good half an hour its runs were certainly less frequent and they were becoming progressively shorter and shorter. Though it stayed deep throughout I was at last getting the measure of this very large fish and looking forward to seeing its bulk. Then as with so many others before, the line parted. Mark was as sick as I was. I recovered all the loose line to see that yet again those unseen rocks on the ocean floor had given the shark the chance of fighting

Enjoying a short scrappy fight with a small lemon of 50 lb on one of the lighter outfits.

Facing page: Mark suggested that my second big lemon should be hauled into the boat and taken back to Banjul, where its flesh is much appreciated.

In this fishing village south of Banjul, everyone turns out to help the boats in with their night's catch of sharks, rays and guitar fish.

173

Following a crash course in wobbling spoons along the Upper Wensum, Tania's daughter, Hannah, graduates with a chunky 12 lb pike, rounding off a wonderful fishing year.

once more. For several yards the 50 lb sylcast was shredded and chewed to the extent that we could never have raised the fish to the boat.

During the fight we had drifted over a mile and upon returning to the buoy I pulled up the anchor caught amongst the jagged rocks while Mark cleared the decks of rods and bait before we headed back upriver and through the harbour into the mangroves, towards the mooring at Denton Bridge.

This 40 minute run is always fascinating, coloured by the array of exotic birds which inhabit the mangroves; but this last trip had a very special feeling about it. It was as though every bird which scratches a living from the swamps had come to say goodbye: noisy pied kingfishers which follow the boat and chatter as they go from tree to tree, herons by the score in grey and white, and the enormous goliath heron standing six feet high with a stork-like beak and a wing span of fully eight feet; colourful nectar-sipping birds, ospreys, pelicans, dunlin, curlews, redshanks, greenshanks. They were all there for us to admire as the sun slowly sank in the western sky, bathing everything in golden light. Overhead, presiding over land and water, the opportunistic vultures were riding the thermals with angelic grace.

It was my last long look at the wonderful watershed of the Gambia River and I savoured it all slowly. Late tomorrow we will be back in the UK and I will have different fishing thoughts on my mind. Perhaps it is always best to leave a place wishing you could experience more; that's certainly how I feel about The Gambia.

Thank you Mark. I hope our programmes do justice both to this fascinating country and to you.

Sunday 2

Overcast and chilly.

I feel guilty, not having wet a line since returning from the Gambian shoot over two weeks back, but then as the run-up towards Christmas in the tackle shop always keeps me busy there is rarely an opportunity to put in any amount of serious fishing at this time of the year. Consequently this morning's light-hearted session was just what the doctor ordered.

Having seen some of the 'off-line cuts' of our Gambian programmes featuring barracuda, Tania's 15-year-old

daughter, Hannah, decided that she fancied a go at catching pike and so after a late breakfast we visited the local mill pool. This part of the River Wensum contains a good head of most species, including a prolific number of jacks. The bottom of the pool is paved with them, as is the wide stretch immediately above the mill. With the river low and running clear I decided that lure fishing would provide enough action for Hannah on such a still, but rather chilly morning.

My good friend, Geoff Atkinson, who owns the mill has two young sons, John and Edward, two large long-haired German shepherds, five extremely friendly Rhode Island red chickens, not to mention a Jack Russell called Millie, and the gang was at the ready to accompany us upriver. Whilst Tania did her best to stop the chickens and dogs from chewing the packs of deadbaits brought along as insurance in case lures failed to produce, I gave Hannah a run down of the pool's depths and gravel bars, suggesting where pike might be lying.

From the first three casts came two lively jacks, both around 4 lb, but a further half hour of trying both lures and wobbled deadbaits produced not a single follow. So it was all back to the mill house for a cuppa and then a sortie upstream along the wide stretch. The first one hundred yards above the sluices failed to produce but from the top of the stretch overhung by old willows and thick beds of sedges came three pike in the space of 10 minutes to an orange and gold spoon. The best, weighing slightly more than 12 lb, gave Hannah a lively scrap in the clear, shallow water which it thrashed to foam each time she bullied it close in, while the dogs ran along the bank barking at the unseen waterbound intruder. Millie, the Jack Russell, became so excited that she flung herself in after the pike and had to be yanked out by the scruff of her neck because of the high bank. What a lovely couple of hours and what a happy ending to a super year's fishing.